# FIRST-TIME MOM:

## What to Expect When You're Expecting

*A New Mom's Survival Guide to Prepare Yourself for Pregnancy, Labor, Childbirth, and New Born Baby*

### By Kate Olsen

# Table of Contents

# Introduction

Congratulations on purchasing this audiobook titled: "First-Time Mom: What to Expect When You're Expecting" and thank you for doing so!

The following chapters will discuss about every aspect of during and after the pregnancy: Expecting, Labor, Childbirth and Newborn. The information found in this book will best explore all you need to learn in order to experience a Healthy Pregnancy. It's your new mom's Survival Handbook.

Thanks again for choosing this audiobook! Every effort was made to ensure it is full of as much useful information as possible.

Please enjoy!

Every woman wants to fulfill her role of becoming a mother to her child. She dreams of carrying her unborn and giving birth to a healthy infant. There is something about first time pregnancy that makes it different and memorable. Nothing can compare to the excitement and anticipation of first time moms to conceive the bundle of her joy.

Along with the fervor of becoming a first time mom, you may feel a little confused, anxious, and fearful. The big responsibility of ensuring the good health and survival of the life inside your womb awaits you. To do so, you should prepare your body to give your unborn the healthy environment he/she needs to live.

It is easy to center your attention to the life inside your womb. You have to remember, though, that your unborn depends heavily on your own health and well-being. It is therefore essential that you have a body ready for pregnancy. Since this is your first time, you may need all the help you can get from your spouse, family, and friends.

You will also find valuable resources online. This pregnancy guide intends to help you how to take good care of yourself for your baby from conception to childbirth. Written for first time moms, it covers everything you need to know in preparing your body before, during, and after your pregnancy. This is the ultimate baby care guide for first time moms like you.

# Chapter 1: A Guide To First-Time Moms

So you want to be a good mom? Don't worry. You will be! You just need to know what to expect. This chapter is all about letting you know what you're in for –and while it's natural to be nervous about the whole thing, preparing for it will ensure that you and your baby will be healthy and happy.

First-time moms are in for a different kind of experience once a baby enters their life. It doesn't even start after delivery–it starts once you see those two pink lines confirming that you have a life in your womb. You'll experience a slew of emotions - - a mixture of excitement, happiness, fear, and many others. It's normal to be nervous. You'd even find yourself worrying a bit about pains during delivery. Aside from that, the imagination of a first-time mom usually goes into overdrive. You might find yourself thinking about the foreseeable future and worrying about whether you can give your baby a good life.

Emotions run high and you'll tend to be extra sensitive during pregnancy, thanks to hormones, which is why you really need to understand your needs and how your body works, and the changes that will occur–from the subtle to the not-so-subtle. If you do that, first-time pregnancy and parenting will be manageable.

The joys of pregnancy and parenthood are overwhelming, but pregnancies also come with a need for a great deal of work, patience, love, support, and understanding. Here are some of the challenges, reminders, and pieces of advice that you should consider so you will enjoy this new stage of your life.

## What To Expect When You're Expecting

Conception, pregnancy, childbirth, and child rearing are no walk in the park. It's easy to say you want to have a baby, but once the baby is there, you discover how hard reality bites. Here are some expectations you need to be ready for:

## The Pains of Childcare

Childcare will definitely burn your energy especially the first few years, and more so, the first few months. You should be ready for sleep interruptions during the night. You will get exhausted during the day may not have enough energy to look after the baby at night. Once you're back to work, you have that to worry about too. You might want to consider asking for a more flexible shift at work. If that isn't possible, hire a nanny who can look after your child. It is going to be worth it. Nothing compares to the feeling of waking up and staying late just staring at the little angel.

## Set Your Priorities

Once you're confirmed that a baby is on the way, it's time to readjust your priorities. This is the first thing you have to remember—you should not try to be a superwoman. You don't have to make sure that your house is spotless, that you serve well-planned healthy meals all the time, maintain your relationships with all friends and work full-time all while taking care of your baby. You have to be realistic about what can be done without stretching yourself too thin. Find out what's more important to you and build your schedule around that. Perhaps, you don't have to keep the place spotless. Perhaps, eating outa few nights a week is okay. You don't even have to completely stick to a rigid schedule. Part of being a parent is thinking on your feet.

Establish a support system

You are going to be your child's anchor but it doesn't hurt to get support from other people, as well. Remember what they say about how it takes a village to raise a child. You don't need a literal village to help you out–you can just ask friends or family not exactly for help but for support. Ask someone over for dinner so you and your child can get some socialization with people other than each other. Also, contrary to popular belief, you can actually endear yourself to someone by asking for help–especially if it's something as easy as help with moving the couch. Even something as simple as calling your own parents to talk about how things are with your child is a good way to establish that support system.

Stay Healthy

Motherhood is going to take a lot of energy so staying fit is important. You should never forget to take care of yourself. That way, you can take care of your child and their needs. Motherhood is a 24/7 job, and you can't afford to get sick or fall to a serious condition because a tiny human being is now dependent on you. Still, you do need some time off to take care of your personal needs, which is why you'll need a readjustment of priorities and a decent support system.

It's challenging–but rewarding -- to be a first-time mom. There will be ups and downs, but if you are determined to take on the challenge, you'll find that it can be fun and exciting –even wondrous at times. Parenthood becomes even more meaningful once you start teaching your child the value of respect, love, and responsibility –and just how to be a good human being in general.

# Chapter 2: Things You Need to Consider When Preparing for Pregnancy

When you get pregnant, your body goes through major changes. You might think that all the changes hormones brought during puberty were enough to make you crazy but just wait until they get to work during your pregnancy! Hence, it's crucial that prepare physically and also mentally. The physical aspect is a given, of course. After all, you'll be nourishing a life inside you. But you see, pregnancy is bound to catapult you into something you may not be quite prepared for. Yes, you expect to get pregnant someday and you might have even been fervently wishing for it. Whatever the case may be, expectation can be quite different from reality; thus, the need to prepare yourself mentally.

You may need to consider your career. This consideration goes hand-in-hand with finances, which is also a crucial part of being a parent. You'd want to make sure that your baby's needs are taken care of. There are some important questions that you will need to ask yourself. How quickly do you intend to get back to work? How do you manage your career and a baby? Pregnancy doesn't come free. In fact, it is expensive. Can you afford to leave your job and risk going through mental stress while trying to think of how you can make ends meet and sustain your pregnancy? Bear in mind the medical bills, the cost of having the baby, baby needs and supplies, and even your own needs. That's why it's important to prepare yourself mentally for the pregnancy challenge.

The next thing you need to work on is preparing your body for pregnancy. As mentioned in the beginning, your body will undergo changes before, during, and after the pregnancy. Therefore, it's important to make sure that your body stays healthy through the entire process. The first thing you need to do is to optimize your weight. You want to enter your pregnancy in the pink of health, so you need to ensure that you are neither overweight nor underweight. Start maintaining a healthy diet. Consult your obstetrician for help on this regard or ask her if she can refer you to a nutritionist. If you were a smoker, now's the best time to quit.

Smoking can lead to low birth weight for your baby, premature labor, and a plethora of other health problems for both you and the baby, not to mention that it can make conceiving a baby difficult in the first place because of the fertility problems it brings. Avoid cigarettes and secondhand smoke.

You may also prepare your body for the pregnancy by taking supplements and prenatal vitamins. Vitamins rich in folic acid and iron are vital, and you would do well to take these in large quantities once pregnant.

# Chapter 3: Making it Through the Pregnancy

Keys to a Happy Healthy Pregnancy

It is ideal to start the lifestyle changes discussed in this chapter even before you become pregnant. But don't worry if you have not done it yet. You can always decide to adopt these changes as soon as you can.

Stay active.

Regular exercise will not only be good for you but for your growing baby, as well. It is important that you stick to a regular routine so you can ensure that your placenta grows big enough to supply oxygen and other nutrients to your baby. Regular exercise can also help keep your heart and your baby's heart in good condition. There have been many studies published to prove that women who remain active and exercise regularly have shorter, less painful deliveries.

Choose an activity that you find enjoyable. There is one basic principle you need to adhere to: always listen to your body. Don't do a particular exercise when it does not feel right. Don't attempt to beat your personal record or finish a marathon during your pregnancy.

Reduce toxins.

• Eat as much real and organic food as you can. Stay away from BPA and canned and processed foods.

• Stop using personal care products that include "parfum" or "fragrance" as ingredients. You can always choose products that have natural essential oils.

- Try making your own cleaning products or use natural ones such as castile soap, baking soda, essential oils and vinegar.

Eat whole foods.

It is ideal for you to eat a well-balanced diet that consists of sufficient amounts of vegetables, fruits, healthy fats and protein. Include a lot of leafy green vegetables in your diet because they are rich in vitamin B and folate, which reduces your baby's risks of neural tube defects.

Sufficient rest.

Your pregnant body needs sufficient sleep so that it will be able to revitalize itself from the higher demands of your growing baby. Even excessive worries and negative thoughts can drain you of physical energy. During the 1st trimester, you may have to sleep extra hours every day to allow your body to adjust to your pregnancy. Try taking a nap or a rest at any time in the day. Try to rest as much as you can.

Consider chiropractic care.

Getting chiropractic care during your entire pregnancy can remove interferences to your nervous system. It can relieve the tension in your back from carrying extra weight, as well as help in readjusting your posture. This can enhance the uterine function and overall development of your baby. It can also help balance your pelvis and remove unnecessary tension that is placed on your ligaments and muscles. Chiropractic care can also improve the positioning of your baby which can allow you to have better natural birth.

Educate yourself.

When you start announcing your pregnancy, a lot of people will start to give their unsolicited advice. They do not really mean harm but sometimes your family and friends can give you the wrong information. This is why it is very important that you perform your own research to see if any information, or any prescribed tests are truly necessary and if they have any side effects that you need to be aware of. Always keep in mind that you have the ultimate responsibility for your baby and every decision that is made is yours to make. Do not let anyone pressure you into something that you do not want to do, and do not feel guilty for your decisions.

Take dietary supplements.

Here are some of the dietary supplements you can consider taking during your pregnancy:

•        Omega-3 which is important for the growth and development of your baby. It is also vital for the proper development of your baby's brain and nervous system. Make sure to ask your doctor which specific supplement is ideal for you to take.

•        Vitamin D is important in reducing your risks of developing a lot of complications related to pregnancy, particularly gestational diabetes. Vitamin D is critical in the proper development of your baby's hormones, bones and muscles. It can also boost your own immune system while pregnant.

•        Probiotics are important in helping your unborn baby obtain sufficient amounts of good bacteria that can help lower their risks of illnesses during the formative years.

•      Folic acid allows the body to create new cells easier. During pregnancy, it can help increase the rate at which your baby develops. It can also help to ensure that your baby's lungs mature easier at the end of your pregnancy.

•      DHA is important to your baby's brain development and it is important for establishing normal brain function. This is a vitamin that is important during pregnancy, and essential for your baby after he is born.

•      Iodine is a vitamin that is typically overlooked. Iodine is important for your baby's brain development during pregnancy and when you are breastfeeding. Since the type and amount of fish that you can eat is limited during this time, it is important that you seek it out elsewhere.

Prenatal Care

Prenatal care is extremely important to your unborn baby. This care allows your doctor to monitor what is going on with your baby while he is still in your tummy.

Prenatal care helps ensure that you and your baby remain as healthy as possible, and that any health conditions are taken care of in a timely manner. Your doctor will also be able to give you care advice that is customized to your individual needs, and what your baby needs.

Every woman, and her pregnancy is different. Even if you have been pregnant before, this pregnancy will be completely different. Therefore, you should treat this pregnancy as what it is, unique.

Most doctors recommend that you be seen in their office for prenatal care using the following schedule:

- Once a month for from the time you are one month pregnant until you are seven months pregnant.

- Two times per month from the time you are seven months pregnant until you are eight months pregnant.

- Every week from the time you are eight months pregnant, until you deliver.

At your prenatal visits, your doctor will do several things, including a physical exam and order lab work.

You can expect the following things to happen at some point in your pregnancy:

- Check your blood pressure at every visit.

- Determine how much weight you have gained.

- Measure your belly to see how much baby has grown.

- Check your baby's heart rate.

- Determine whether you have a family history of disorders that may affect your pregnancy.

- A physical exam, including a pelvic exam.

- Blood based laboratory tests.

- Answer any questions you may have about your changing body.

How You Can Prepare for Doctor Visits

Over the next eight months, you and your doctor will become very close. Your doctor will be your go to person for questions and concerns that you have during your pregnancy. They are a great resource, but only if you handle this relationship in the right manner. Here is some amazing advice to ensure that you get the most out of this relationship.

Select the Right Doctor

By choosing the right doctor, you are doing you and your baby a huge favor. When getting your needed medical care you should take the step to create a solid relationship as doctor and patient. You should also make sure that you feel the doctor you choose to see is compassionate and competent. Mary Jane Minkin, MD says "Trust is one of the most important factors in a good doctor-patient relationship."

Mary Jane Minkin is a clinical professor of gynecology and obstetrics at the School of Medicine at the Yale University. You and your doctor should be comfortable with each other. There should be no tension when he walks in the room or if you think he is mistreating you. If you think this is happening to you than you should try to find another midwife, doctor, or a new health care provider. You need to make sure that you find some one you click with and stay with them. Because there are so many legal issues there are a lot of doctors that are retiring from the field of obstetrics. This means that many of them have gone to being OB's.

Ask questions (within reason)

If this is your first time being pregnant than you no doubt have lots of questions. If you do than you most definitely should ask them. Just remember you only have so much time so try to ask a reasonable amount of questions. Make sure that you prioritize your most important questions so that you can ask a few at a time. This will make sure you get your most important questions answered first.

Write down your questions--and the answers

One of the most important things you can do when you have questions is to write them down in a notebook. This will make sure you don't forget what your questions were and you can take them with you to make sure you ask your doctor. You can also take your notebook with you so that when you ask your questions you can write down what the doctor has to say about it. This way you will have them with you all the time.

Tell your doctor at the start of your appointment that you have questions

Doctors have many preferences in when they like to ask you if you have any questions. Some will ask in the beginning or at the end. The ones that ask in the beginning of an appointment like to make sure that if it is something they need to check during the exam. You can also let them know in the beginning that there are things that you want to go over that might need checked during the exam.

Save late-night calls for emergencies

It is important to save questions that are not an emergency for your regular visits instead of taking up the doctors' time. Or you can call the office during business hours and ask questions.

Talk to the nurse

You can call your doctors office and talk to the nurse if you have any questions between appointments. There are some questions that nurses can answer immediately. This will keep you from having to wait on the doctor calling you back for an answer that the nurse could have given you. If the nurse can't answer your question they can arrange for the doctor to call you back.

Don't come spouting facts from the Internet

You can find some answers online. If you search the internet it helps to look for the websites that are legitimate medical sites. Also if you read something you should ask your doctor if what you read is true or not. You should not jump to conclusions from the internet and tell the doctor that what you read makes you think that you should have a C-section. Saying something like this can make your doctor become defensive and in turn making appointments intense.

Show that you're invested in your pregnancy

Here is one of the ways that you can help show your doctor that you really care and are going to invest time into your pregnancy. If you are a smoker and you choose to quit when you first find out that you are pregnant. This will allow the doctor to see that you truly care about the health of your baby and that your pregnancy goes more smoothly. This will make your life and the doctors life that much easier. The more effort you put into doing things right for your pregnancy the more the doctor will be willing to help you.

People will tell you throughout your pregnancy that you are glowing. It's true, you are. Pregnancy skin shines and you are beautiful. There are going to be times when you feel unbelievably womanly and graceful. You will feel like you could be Mother Earth herself. Truth time here. There are probably going to be more times that you feel like something the cat drug in. Pregnancy is hard. Truth time again. Morning sickness does not happen to everyone and some people barely get it. Some of you though are going to get it and get it bad. Holding down food, at least for the first few months, is going to be a memory for you.

Crackers do help. Ingesting a small handful of crackers before getting up out of bed in the morning can be a big help. It is important to eat small meals. If you start to feel like you are a little queasy or a little full then it is time to stop. You can always eat more later on! You are going to be thirsty when you are pregnant and it is very important for the sake of both you and the baby to stay well hydrated. However, when you have morning sickness do not guzzle water. If you drink too fast it is going to come back up. Just take small sips and you will have a much better chance to keep everything down.

Another good choice for morning sickness? Ginger! Some people drink ginger ale and some people take a ginger supplement. Another yummy way to do it is gingersnaps! They really do work but be careful not to scarf too many down at once. You don't want them coming back up!

For most pregnant women morning sickness does go away after the first three months. After that, if your sickness is gone, you may get very hungry! And yes, it is true, you will crave food. Cravings can be very hardcore! Don't be surprised if you burst into tears one day and cry your eyes out because the local mini mart is out of beef jerky or chocolate doughnuts. One month you may want nothing but steak lots of steak. Another month, meat may turn your stomach inside out and all you want to eat is cantaloupe. There is no rhyme or reason to it that's for sure!

Some foods you do need to avoid in pregnancy. You probably were not going to eat it anyway but no raw or undercooked meat. No rare steak for you girl! This does include fish so if you love sushi you will have to bid it farewell for a while. Oysters and clams are both a big no no. Eggs are ok but make sure to check that are pasteurized and cook them fully before eating. Truth time. No one likes to admit but a lot of people like raw cookie dough. In pregnancy though you are going to have to bake those cookies, raw cookie dough is definitely not allowed!

Your body and your mind is going to change. Having a child growing inside you is flat out amazing. Hearing the heartbeat for the first time is indescribable. You will feel emotions that you did not even know you were capable of having. A fierce protectiveness for the unborn child will seem to come out of nowhere. You will protect your stomach while out in public without even noticing you are doing it. One day you will feel a tiny flutter and wonder what if, this usually happens around month four, but the next flutter will be stronger and you will know without a doubt. It is your child in there moving and growing and kicking.

Your hair may look more lustrous and that is good because you are not allowed to dye it while you are pregnant. Your partner is most likely going to find you extremely sexy and believe it or not your sex drive is going to soar. If you were wondering, yes you can have sex while you are pregnant. You might even want to have a lot of it because the first few months after the baby is born are guaranteed to turn into a dry spell. If you experience any cramping or spotting after sex make sure to discuss this with your doctor. You are going to start to love your baby bump and continue to love it even as you grow. You will sing to your baby and people will say hello to the little one through your belly button. (Whether or not you want them to!) These changes are truly amazing!

Truth time. Not all the changes can be classified as amazing, in fact some or downright annoying and uncomfortable. Heartburn you should expect. Mothers that have never had heartburn will start to have it. Anything can cause it too, even sugar! It is unpleasant. Small meals and sleeping on pillows (so you aren't lying flat) can make a huge difference. Your boobs are going to get bigger, possibly a lot bigger! Yes, this can be nice. However, you will probably be surprised to see your nipples leaking. Months before your milk comes in, your colostrum can start to leak, this is normal! Colostrum is the thick creamy nourishment your baby will drink for the first few days of her life. So, if you see some leakage from your nipples, do not fear! If it worries you then calling your doctor is always a viable option.

In fact, do not forget that is why your doctor is there! Call their office anytime day or night when you are worried about something. It is their job to take care of you!

The more your baby grows the more your body stretches. Babies are so small you wouldn't think that your body would stretch too much, right? Wrong! The ligaments that run from your naval up to your ribs are going to hurt and at times they are going to hurt very badly. Getting off your feet whenever possible is always a smart decision. The longer you stand the more you are going to feel the stretch. There are products out there you can take advantage of. A belly belt is kind of like a girdle only it holds your baby up instead of your stomach in. The choice to use one of these is completely up to you. Most likely you will find yourself unconsciously holding your baby up long before you deliver him. The tiny precious feet you are so looking forward to kissing or going to feel monstrous when they are in your ribs. Not only do all babies like to move and kick but they have some sort of sixth sense about kicking mommy directly in the ribs or jumping up and down on mama's bladder.

Speaking of bladders. Truth time again. There is a good chance you may pee your pants at some point. At the very least trickle. The last couple months of pregnancy the baby is growing rapidly towards full term size. Your internal organs fit inside you quite nicely before you got pregnant. Do they go anywhere when you are pregnant? Oh no! They just get squished! One day when you are nine months pregnant you are going to cough and see just how squished your bladder really is!

Sleep may be difficult, especially near the end. If you were a belly sleeper before you have some adjusting to do. Have you ever tried to sleep on your stomach with a beach ball underneath you? It just does not work. Anytime you can rest though take full advantage of it. Labor and delivery is coming and your body needs to be ready to handle it.

# Chapter 4: First Trimester: What They Don't Tell You

The first trimester of pregnancy is really an introduction period for your body and the new baby. Much is going on inside you and changes are happening to make room for the baby to grow. And get all of the nutrients it needs to mature into a full term fetus. The first trimester is the moment of conception up to the 12th week, or the 3rd month. For many women this is the most difficult trimester of them all. Your body is making a lot of adjustments.

The experience during first trimester varies for all women. You may not feel pregnant or then again you may feel very pregnant. Some women say that they have a full feeling inside of their stomachs from the very moment they conceive. Others even swear they know the exact moment that the baby was conceived. While there are no medical tests that can confirm a pregnancy this early, it is very much possible for a woman to have this type of experience.

It is hard to know for sure what you will experience or how intense your experience will be. Heartburn, morning sickness, being uncomfortable and nauseated -- these are all things that are commonly experienced by pregnant women during the first trimester.

What is the truth of the matter? Sometimes these experiences can be very difficult, and even if you have experienced them before pregnancy, these experiences are more intense during pregnancy. Heartburn is maximized 10 times over; your body is hot and you feel bloated. Even the smell of water makes you want to run to the bathroom to vomit. Morning sickness, even when you do not actually vomit, can cause pure misery. And, has anyone warned you about dry heaves? These are a few of the common experiences that occur during your first trimester.

Morning Sickness & More

Morning sickness should really have a new name because it is very misleading. It is sickness all right, but it does not discriminate and it causes trouble in more than just the morning. For some pregnant women morning sickness can be absolutely horrible, disrupting life in every single way. These women cannot stay out of the bathroom, and sometimes it is not that they are throwing up, but that they feel as if they want to 24 hours a day. It is not a pretty picture that we are painting here, and that is because there is nothing pretty about morning sickness. It can occur morning, noon and night, and sometimes it occurs during all three and never goes away. A package of saltines on hand to bite on when morning sickness strikes is the new-mom secret. A Sprite or ginger ale can also do the trick to ease your sickness. Do not think that you will only have mild nausea in the morning and it will all go away. This is one of the marks of pregnancy and most women will have it. And, chances are that it is going to be pretty severe for the first trimester. If you do not experience morning sickness, or if it is something that you experience only in mild form, then you are very lucky.

If you normally do not go to the bathroom very often, then get ready for that to change after pregnancy. The bathroom is your best friend during your pregnancy. Going there will be something that you have to do often! As soon as you wash your hands and get comfortable on the couch, you will have to go again. There's a lot of pressure with a baby sitting on your bladder, even if it does only weigh a half an ounce. The problem with frequent urination is that it doesn't go away until the pregnancy is over. In fact, the bigger baby gets, the worse the problem gets, too.

## Heartburn, Acne & More

Heartburn is also something that you probably will experience during the first trimester. It is one of the most common side effects during pregnancy. Women who are pregnant with multiples report that the heartburn is even worse. However, most women with child will experience heartburn, and it really burns. It is a good idea to go ahead and get a bottle of Tums and expect to chew them like candy. You can drink water to help ease heartburn as well.

Even if you have been lucky enough to have never had a pimple before in your life, the hormonal changes with pregnancy may very well bring on an outbreak. For many women in their first trimester acne is a big concern. Many pregnant women fear using the products sold over the counter to get rid acne, scared that it will harm the baby. However, there are numerous home remedies for acne available that are perfectly safe for both mom and baby, while also being effective at eliminating acne breakouts. Some women experience no breakouts, some a few pimples and zits, and other women have full blown breakouts, and again, this is not something that anyone can determine ahead of time. If it does affect you, the key is to be prepared and ready to treat. If you do want to help keep your skin looking its very best, make sure that you wash the face twice per day, using a gentle soap or a mild cleanser. Follow up with a moisturizer to keep the skin soft. You can also talk to your doctor about acne treatments if you do not want to use those that are sold over the counter. Your doctor can give you many other tips and tricks to help combat acne as well.

You are going to be tired. Really tired. No matter how much you sleep it will never seem as if you have had enough. And, when you are awake you are probably not going to be jumping up and down and full of energy. Pregnancy takes a lot out of you. Make plans to settle down just a little bit, compared to your normal activities, that is. While you do not have to sit in the house and do nothing but protect your belly all day, you do need to make a few exceptions, avoid a few things and prepare for those days when staying in bed. You are not going to be getting a lot of sleep in nine months, and you are going to want it. So, go ahead and take advantage of it now, and sleep in when you can and put some of the normal activities to the side. The most important things that you can do right now is take care of your body and the new baby that is growing inside of you, and one of the things that you can do is get the extra sleep that you need.

An Emotional Roller Coaster

Aside from those kinds of changes, expect your emotions to be up and down. Many would suspect you were bipolar if they did not know you were pregnant. The smallest of things can cause an emotional meltdown -- and we do mean a meltdown. Uncontrollable crying isn't uncommon, and expect to be ultra-sensitive. You may cry over every single movie that you see, and something as crazy as getting a hamburger with a pickle on it can send you into frenzy. Your body is going through many changes. It isn't your fault; it is all of those hormones that your body is accumulating.

Mood changes are very common. One minute you are fine and the next you are not. It is just a part of pregnancy. This is first seen in the first trimester, but it is one of those things that continue throughout the entire pregnancy.

Here are a few other very important things that you need to know about pregnancy in the first trimester.

1. You will also worry about everything. What if you fall while walking down the street? What if something is wrong with the

baby? Are you going to be a good mother? Will you produce enough breast milk? What are the best diapers? While seemingly irrational to the non-pregnant brain, prepare to worry about the smallest, sillier of things as if they were a major life decision. Just remember, this too shall pass. It is not uncommon for pregnant women to worry about everything. It is a new experience and there is a lot that is going on inside of your body, after all.

2. During the first trimester you might also notice veins in your body that you have never noticed before. This is not uncommon and many women experience this. Whether in your arms or legs, veins seem to pop out of nowhere.

3. Noticing that your legs are a little hairier than they usually are, or that your hair is back the day after you shave? Again this is something that you should plan for and prepare for, because for most pregnant women it happens. Pregnancy is one of the healthiest times in the world, as long as you take care of yourself, and this means that hair (everywhere on the body) is growing rapidly. The hair on top of your head will also have this same effect. If you have thin hair, ordinarily expect to get a totally new mane that you will absolute love.

Your Doctor Visits

There is little change that comes during the first trimester physically, and chances are that most people will not even realize that you are pregnant. Although they say that you cannot feel baby move around until many weeks into the pregnancy, it is very much possible to feel butterflies in the stomach, which is the baby. This is just something that you know when you feel it. It is certainly a feeling like nothing else in this world.

The doctor will see you once a month during the first trimester, and sometime during the 8th week he will listen for a heartbeat. This is an amazing sound to hear. Some doctors will record it for you if you would like, and this is definitely an amazing memory to have to hold. Your doctor will also give you a due date, a date of conception and a ton of information to take home with you and read, including pregnancy magazines.

Most moms would tell you to read these books and learn as much as you can, and you should. But, at the same time, remember that you need to give yourself leeway and rarely does a pregnancy happen just as they predict in those magazines. Every woman will have her own unique experience and this is all a part of the enjoyment of being pregnant. Learn from the books and magazines and do all that you can to abide by the rules and the tips that they offer. But at the same time, do not make the mistake of thinking that everything is going to happen just like it says in those books.

And, another tip, do not throw all of those advertisements away. You are still new to being pregnant, and you are still unaware of just what it means to be a new mom. But, the pregnancy companies out there do and they are ready to help you out. Baby will drink a massive amount of formula, and at a cost of about $30 a can, this can get expensive quickly. Add to that the cost of diapers and you have a very expensive new life forming inside of you. It is all worth it, but you might as well take advantage of all of the help that you can get. Many of those advertisements that you see in magazines are for baby clubs. It is a good idea to go ahead and join them now. You will get plenty of full size products in the mail and lots of extra goodies, too. This can include  diaper bags, bottles, wipes, formula, birth announcements, photos and more. You never know what kind of offers that you will find inside, but join all of the clubs that you can!

# Chapter 5: What To Expect During The Second Trimester

Week 13

This is the onset of the second trimester, and your baby is now at 7.5cm in length and 25 grams in weight, which is actually the size of a peach. The skeletal part of your baby's body begins to develop starting with the collar (clavicle) and thigh (femur) bones. Also, your baby starts to turn its head, swallow and hiccup. The baby can also kick their legs. The baby's stomach and vocal cord start to develop at the 13th week. In addition, your baby starts to take his first breath. The blood from the umbilical cord supplies the oxygen, and with a closer look it will seem as though your baby is breathing under water.

For you, you should be back to your normal self with minimal episodes of morning sickness, and the good news is that your chances of having a miscarriage is now a low probability. Also, you should notice a little more expansion of your waistline and bust.

Week 14

Your baby is becoming bigger and stronger at this stage. The arms are fully grown in proportion to the rest of the body while the legs are still undergoing growth. The baby's length is 8cm (about half a banana) while the current weight should be around 42 grams. The baby has hair and the eyebrows are formed before the end of this week. One surprising development process that occurs at this stage is the development of your baby's fingerprints. The baby will also start sucking their thumb. Also, your baby will start making use of their facial muscles to make expressions like squinting, frowning and grimacing.

You may suffer occasional forgetfulness as a result of the pregnancy hormones in your body. Also, nose bleeding is to be expected at this stage and you will experience a huge craving for food.

Week 15

Remember that I mentioned earlier that the baby's head was a third of its entire body. The good news is that by this fifteenth week, your baby's head must have grown into proportion with the rest of the body. The baby is 11.5cm (about the size of an orange) long, and his ears are fully developed at this stage to hear sounds. The baby will also grow some fine downy hair referred to as lanugo meant to keep the baby warm until they are able to develop a layer of subcutaneous fat to keep them warm after birth. The baby's sucking, swallowing and gasping skills have also advanced and will probably have developed their taste buds. The baby can also hear your voice by now so you should try to sing to them or talk to them often.

Although your baby's eyelids should still be closed at the moment, he can recognize lights. For instance, if you put a flashlight directly on your belly, you will feel some movements; that is your baby moving away from the light.

You will notice a dark line from your navel and down your abdomen and your baby bump starts getting noticeable.

Week 16

Your baby is probably the size of an avocado. At this stage, your baby's joints and limbs should be fully developed. Their backbone is also a lot stronger and they have probably mastered the art of sucking the thumb. Also, your baby's nervous system starts to connect with other muscles that will help your baby's movements. I talked about your baby developing skin much earlier. The skin at this stage is so transparent that you can clearly see the tiny veins underneath the skin. Their facial muscles are also a lot more developed so their expressions are a lot more visible although the baby doesn't yet know how to control them. The baby will also develop the ability to grab and play with the umbilical cord.

Your libido increases considerably. You will find yourself feeling the urge to have sex more often than usual. You can have as much sex as you want at this period without harming your baby. All you need to do is to find a comfortable sex position since your bump might get in the way.

Week 17

Your baby weighs around 150g in this week, and his or her facial features are fully developed. You may start feeling some firm movements in your womb. Your baby's brain begins to regulate the heartbeat to 140 to 150 beats per minute, which is still twice your own heartbeat. Meanwhile, your baby's fingerprints become more pronounced at this stage.

You will start feeling more energetic and less tired than you have in the past weeks. Now is the time to make use of that energy. Get the baby's room ready, take a workout class for pregnant mothers or join a walking group. Get out there and put that energy to good use! Getting more physically active now will help greatly later on, trust me!

Week 18

Your baby at this stage has grown to 14cm, and weighs almost 200g. The eggs start developing (in a female child), while the nerves begin to build up a protective covering referred to as myelin to enable the nervous system to develop and function properly upon birth. The baby at this period has also been

31

engaged in lots of movements including kicking, tumbling and rolling. Their grip is also developed. The baby is also able to hold their umbilical cord firmly when playing.

Meanwhile, you tend to add more weight as the days go by. This is a combination of your weight, your baby's weight, the amniotic fluid, and the placenta.

Week 19

Your baby weighs about 240g and is about 14cm long at this stage. The baby's weight is more than that of the placenta now. Your baby's legs have grown into proportion with the rest of his body while the cartilage continues to harden. The baby's skin becomes less translucent and the skin pigments, which will determine the color of your baby's skin, will start to form. The baby will also start developing the Vernix Caseosa (this is the waxy or cheese-like white substance that coats your baby's skin when he or she is born) on its body to protect its body from the side effects of his contact with amniotic acid. The baby will also start developing some hair on its scalp, although the hair at this stage will be white and pigment free since the baby's hair color is yet to be determined. The baby can hear you well at this time.

You will notice a considerable increase in your bump size. Also heartburn and indigestion will be some of the symptoms that may occur during this period.

Week 20

Your baby is entering his fifth month this week. He or she will grow stronger and bigger to 16.5 cm length size; about the size of a banana but growing pretty fast. Also, at this stage, the part of the brain that controls the senses will start developing to help your baby to taste, see, touch and smell.

Your baby will also start producing something referred to as Meconium, within their bowel. Meconium refers to a harmless mixture of the amniotic fluid, which the baby has swallowed already, coupled with dead skin cells and digestive secretions. This mixture forms the baby's first bowel movement just after birth.

Your back may start aching as your bump continues to get bigger. Also, you may experience pain in your pelvis at this stage in your pregnancy as well.

Week 21

This week, your baby has increased in length to make him or her about 27cm long and weighing about 360g. Although your baby continues to add weight, it still lacks fats in its body. However, they will start adding on some fats that will ultimately give them the chubby 'baby' look when you first see them. The eyebrows have also developed and the eyelids can actually blink at this time.

One good point at this stage is that your baby's taste buds are fully developed to enable them to taste different flavors from the food you eat as they swallow the amniotic fluid. Also, the vernix caseosa is fully developed right now.

You should be making frequent visits to the antenatal ward by now. Antenatal classes help you (and your partner) prepare for labor, birth and early parenthood. You might also be interested in breastfeeding workshops as well.

Week 22

The baby is now about the size of a papaya, about 27cm from head to toe and still growing fast. The body will also keep growing its placenta to provide nourishment for the baby.

The baby at this stage gets his nourishment from the placenta instead of the yolk sac, and his or her gums and tooth bud are in place now. Although your baby's eyes are fully developed, the eyes have no color because of the absence of the pigment in their iris. Your baby has now mapped a sleeping and waking up time for themselves and the pancreas is intact now.

Your major problem at this stage will be your swollen feet and ankles as your baby belly becomes bigger.

Week 23

Your baby looks more like a newborn baby but just smaller. It is now 30cm long and weighs 500g, and its body at this stage has started producing fats, so it will start bulking up from this week. When the baby is very active, you should be able to see him or her moving under your skin. The skin is still translucent such that you can see the bones and organs through the skin. At this age, the baby won't jump as much when exposed to loud noises. You can start playing classical music to sooth them.

You will continue to notice a considerable weight gain in your baby, which is also manifested in your own weight gain.

Week 24

Your baby is 1 foot long, and weighs 600g. Medically, it has been proven that a baby born at this stage (that is prematurely) has a high survival rate. Your baby can detect the sound of your heartbeat and your voice at this stage while his or her eyebrows and hair are fully developed now. Additionally, the baby's lungs have grown such that it can now breathe in actual air rather than fluids (thanks to the production of surfactant. If the baby doesn't produce this substance, it will have some breathing problems) and their face has nicely developed eyebrows, eyelashes and hair, which is still white (lacking pigmentation).

You may experience bleeding in your gums around this time, which is one dental problem that is synonymous with pregnancy.

Week 25

The baby at this time is growing fast. He or she gets to the size of 13 ½ inches long and with a weight of about 1 ½ pounds. The baby also starts plumping up thanks to the buildup of fat deposits under the skin to make them look more like normal. The baby will probably be hyperactive at this period (with such activities like somersaults, and wriggling). They will also be responsive to certain sounds so singing to them wouldn't be a bad idea.

Week 26

Your baby has grown to 2lbs and 35.5cm long, and the eyes are finally open. There is an increase in your baby's brain activity during this period and the testicles (if it is a boy) are descending to his scrotum (this takes 2-3 months to complete). You will probably start experiencing some more contractions, which are similar to menstrual cramps coupled with pain as the developing fetus stretches the uterus. The baby's circulatory system is well developed while the umbilical cord keeps on thickening as it gets stronger to support the supply of various nutrients to the baby.

Week 27

Your baby's weight is at 875g now and his eyesight has developed well enough to differentiate between night and day, but that doesn't mean that your baby will keep to the rule of sleeping in the night. Also, your baby's brain is in the final stage of development now. The baby also hiccups often and will probably do that more often when you eat spicy foods.

Your appetite is likely to increase and you will have cravings for food you don't typically eat as part of your normal diet. Like the famous pickles and ice cream combo.

## Tips To Survive The Second Trimester

Backache

There is extra pressure on your back from carrying your baby. You can ease it off a bit by always using a chair with back support, sleep on your side with a pillow in between your legs and avoid picking heavy items off the ground.

Nosebleeds

The mucous membrane in your nose is swollen because of the hormonal changes taking place in your body, which may lead to constant nosebleeds for you. You need to keep your head up and apply gentle pressure to your nose to stop the bleeding.

Appearance Of Varicose Veins

They appear as a result of an increase in circulation of blood in your body to send blood to the growing fetus. The veins will disappear with time after birth.

Weight Gain

After your morning sickness subsides, your appetite returns in full force. You are likely to gain 1 to 3 pounds every week during this time. You have to work on practicing portion control for whatever you eat.

Nutrition

Vital organs of the body are beginning to develop. As such, you have to continue with foods high in protein and vegetables. Eat more of fiber-filled food to keep you full.

Exercise

With the stop in morning sickness and the regaining of your strength, you can start mild workout regimes, yoga, and meditation to keep fit.

Braxton Hick's Contraction

This is also known as fake contraction, and occurs towards and during the later part of the third trimester. The Braxton hick is a warm up exercise to prepare your uterus for labor. There is nothing much you can do about the fake labor but if it becomes so intense, then you may need to visit the hospital. At this time, you can probably sense some metallic taste in your mouth due to toxins accumulation from the lymphatic system. Don't worry; it will improve with time.

Colostrum leakage

Besides having tender breasts, you will probably start producing colostrum (a liquid from the breasts, which is often clear or creamy yellow with the consistency of syrup) from the 14th to the 16th week. If you notice some blood here, this is probably due to the rapid growth of blood vessels growing in the ductal system as your body preps for breastfeeding. Use breast pads inside your bra to deal with this.

Skin changes

Your skin, hair, and nails might start having changes like pigmentation, stretch marks, red spider veins, hormonal rashes, dry and oily skin, skin tags etc. Worry not because this is completely normal.

Swelling and fluid retention

This is referred to as edema (this starts at around 20 weeks into the pregnancy). You may also notice swellings on your hands, legs, and feet; these often become worse when it is hot. Varicose veins are usually linked to causing swelling. You should try to get your blood pressure tested if your swelling doesn't go away after week 20.

Gestational hypertension

This might happen when you are around 20 weeks pregnant. And if you have gestational hypertension coupled with high protein levels in your urine, you might be suffering from preeclampsia, which is usually characterized with kidney problems, visual changes and headaches.

Note: Having gestational hypertension is likely to make you increase your risk of stillbirth, intrauterine growth restriction, preterm birth, and placental abruption. Get your weight under control because this is closely linked to gestational hypertension.

Gestational diabetes

Ensure to have your blood sugar tested just to help you determine whether you might be having gestational diabetes since suffering from this could put you and the baby at risk. Weight and your diet are key determinants of this. Therefore, making some necessary changes to your diet could minimize your chances of developing such problems.

You will also need to deal with rapid weight gain, weird dreams, itchy breasts, sleeping problems, increased libido and energy, leg cramps, itchy bumps, heartburn, backache and others. These shouldn't be any problem, as they will pass with time.

# Chapter 6: What To Expect In Your Third Trimester

The third trimester is the final trimester of your actual pregnancy! While many believe that pregnancy will continue into a fourth trimester, or your postpartum period, your physical pregnancy will be done by the end of this trimester! That is, you will be giving birth to your baby! This final trimester brings a whole new myriad of symptoms, if you didn't already guess that, but at the same time after all of this practice, you are probably more than ready to manage them!

During the third trimester, you are going to want to be extra cautious of your body, because this is when labor will happen! For some women, labor happens on or after their due date, but for others they can go into early labor. It is important that you stay in tune with your body so you can alert your doctor if any major changes occur. In this chapter, you will learn what normal symptoms are, and what you should look out for! As well, you will learn more about what to expect with your doctors' visits.

SYMPTOMS

The symptoms you will experience in the third trimester are different, but not terribly different, from those you have already experienced. For the most part, they will simply be exaggerated versions of the symptoms you've already been experiencing. However, there are a few additional ones you might experience. You can learn all about it below!

LEG PAINS

This trimester, you are going to continue to experience the leg pains you have already likely been experiencing throughout the second trimester. The larger you get, the more pressure it puts on your legs and it can become very painful. Luckily, these will go away once your baby is born! In the meantime, you should do your best to stay off of your feet for long periods of time. You can also drink coconut milk or eat bananas, which are both rich in potassium, a nutrient that can significantly help reduce leg cramping.

NECK AND SHOULDER PAIN

Your growing belly is putting a lot of forward pressure on your back, which can also affect your neck and shoulders. You may notice your neck and shoulders are feeling just as bad as your lower back feels. This is completely normal. The best thing you can do is take a warm bath (but not hot!), get gentle massages, and relax a lot. If you find that it is affecting your sleep, try using body pillows and other pillows to help you support your back, legs, and belly.

HUNGRY, BUT NOT

A symptom many women report feeling that is extremely uncomfortable is the feeling that they are incredibly hungry, but are not able to eat. This is because your body needs more nutrition in order to support the growing baby. However, because your baby is getting so big, your stomach is running out of room! That means you don't have to eat as much to feel incredibly full. The best way to combat this symptom is to eat high-protein and nutrient rich mini-meals several times throughout the day. This will help keep you full and give your body all of the nutrients it needs without feeling excessively full.

LACK OF BLADDER CONTROL

Many people experience lack of bladder control when they are in their late pregnancy stages. The best thing to do is stay near a washroom, and relieve your bladder regularly. You may also wish to wear a pad if you will be going out, as they help to keep you from accidentally peeing your pants. As well, you may wish to lean forward when you are peeing to help get all of the urine out of your bladder, as the pressure of your baby may prevent you from eliminating your bladder completely.

CONSTIPATION

While your urine may be hard to stop, your bowels may slow down all on their own. This is caused, again, by all of the pressures and hormones going on in your body. You can combat this symptom through eating dates, prunes, and other fiber-rich foods that can help keep things flowing. As well, make sure you're staying hydrated, as that is important for you and your body, and it will help keep things moving.

DOCTOR VISITS AND MEDICAL TESTS

Your third trimester is going to be the most intensive one you will experience in regards to doctors' appointments. Towards the end of your third trimester, you are going to have your doctor visits increase to weekly visits. The exact time this will happen will depend on your doctor, the healthiness of your pregnancy, and whether or not you have been showing any signs of labor.

The doctors' appointments in this trimester will continue to include all of the same things as previous ones did: they will weigh you, measure your abdomen, check your blood pressure and pulse, and take a urine sample to check for protein in the urine. Towards the end of the trimester, you will likely also get pelvic exams to see if your cervix is dilating at all. At the end of each appointment, you will be informed of what to look for in the coming days.

You actually won't experience any medical examinations this trimester, unless you are carrying an at-risk pregnancy. If you have high or low blood pressure, gestational diabetes, or any other pregnancy ailment, your doctor may require you to get an ultrasound or blood test taken to monitor your pregnancy a little more closely. Otherwise, you will not experience any further medical tests!

# Chapter 7: Pregnancy Symptoms You Should Not Ignore

For many women, the third trimester goes all the way through effortlessly. For others, particularly those who are carrying at-risk pregnancies, you might run into a few complications. While your doctor has likely discussed this with you, particularly if you are known to be a high risk pregnancy, it can still be good to have this knowledge on hand. The following symptoms are things you should never avoid during your pregnancy. If any of these occur, you should call your doctor immediately or head to the maternity ward at your hospital.

EXCESSIVE PAIN ANYWHERE IN YOUR BELLY

Experiencing aches and pains is completely normal during pregnancy, especially in the third trimester. As your baby grows more and more, he or she will be running out of room and you may experience pain due to your baby's movement. However, if you are experiencing severe pain that is not related to the baby moving around, regardless of where it is in your stomach, you should call your doctor right away. You should be sure to monitor it especially if this pain persists or won't go away no matter what you do.

A HIGH FEVER WITH NO SYMPTOMS

If you have an extremely high fever but aren't experiencing symptoms of the flu, you should contact your doctor right away. This is not a common symptom late in pregnancy, and could indicate that you are presently fighting an infection. Your doctor will be able to help you confirm an accurate diagnosis and help reduce your fever depending on what he or she discovers.

## EXCESSIVE VISUAL DISTURBANCES

While a slight change in vision is normal during pregnancy, excessive visual disturbances are not. If you are experiencing double vision, blurred vision, dimming or flashing spots, or other lights that are lasting for more than two hours or that are making you feel unwell, you should call your doctor right away. These symptoms are not normal and should be addressed immediately.

## EXTREME SWELLING IN HANDS AND FEET

Swelling due to increased blood volume and fluid retention is normal, but extreme or excessive swelling in your hands and feet are not. If these symptoms appear suddenly or are accompanied by a headache or problems with your vision, you should contact your doctor.

## SEVERE HEADACHE THAT WON'T GO AWAY

If you are experiencing a sudden and bad headache that won't go away after two to three hours, you should contact your doctor. If you are experiencing a headache alongside excessive swelling or visual disturbances, you should call your doctor right away and get seen as soon as possible.

## ANY AMOUNT OF VAGINAL BLEEDING

When labor is about to start, you may experience something called a bloody show. However, if you experience bleeding that is heavy, light, dark, or otherwise abnormal, you should contact your doctor. In the earlier stages of pregnancy, light spotting is usually just implantation bleeding. However, any time after implantation, any amount of blood may be a concern. You should also look out for other symptoms, such as abdominal pain or back pain, which can be a potential sign of miscarriage.

## FLUIDS LEAKING FROM YOUR VAGINA

It is really common for you to experience an increase in cervical discharge, as your body is working harder to keep potential bacteria build up out of your body to prevent infections. However, if you notice a watery fluid leaking from your vagina before 37 weeks, you will need to call your doctor right away. They will likely want to admit you to the hospital to check on your membranes and make sure they haven't ruptured. If they have, they will need to treat you to help prevent infection and prepare you and your baby for a potential premature labor and birth.

## A SUDDEN AND DRAMATIC INCREASE IN THIRST, WITH REDUCED URINATION

Pregnant women are at risk for dehydration, so it is important that you are drinking a lot of water throughout your entire pregnancy. However, if you notice that you are suddenly starting to feel extremely thirsty, and you aren't urinating as often, you will want to talk to your doctor. This can be a symptom of dehydration, or it can be a symptom of gestational diabetes. Your doctor is the only person who can determine the exact cause, so you will need to speak with them to get assistance.

## URINARY TRACT INFECTION SYMPTOMS

Urinary tract infections can be particularly dangerous during pregnancy, so you will want to discuss any UTI symptoms you may experience with your doctor. They will treat you and help ensure that the infection does not affect your uterus or your growing baby.

## SEVERE OR EXCESSIVE VOMITING

Vomiting has the ability to cause dehydration and weakness in anyone, but especially a pregnant mother. While vomiting itself doesn't necessarily indicate anything is wrong, and it won't hurt your baby, you should make sure you keep your doctor in the loop about this. This will help them monitor you and ensure you aren't becoming severely dehydrated. If you are vomiting too much, you may need to be admitted to the hospital to receive fluids in order to keep you hydrated.

If you are later in your pregnancy and start suddenly vomiting an excessive amount, especially with a pain just below the ribs, you should call your doctor right away. This can be a symptom of a few different complications, all of which will need to be treated by a doctor.

## FAINTING OR DIZZINESS

If you haven't eaten enough during the day, you may experience fainting or dizziness. However, it can also be caused by low blood pressure. It is important that you contact your doctor about this symptom if it is persistent, or if you faint at all. They will want to make sure that you are well, and work with you to prevent it from happening again.

## SLOWED DOWN FETAL MOVEMENTS

Most often, your doctor will ask you to monitor fetal movements, to ensure your baby is moving regularly. If at any time you realize you have not felt your baby move in a while, or you perform a kick count and your baby is not as active as normal, you will want to contact your doctor. In most cases, this simply means the baby is resting. However, in some extreme cases, this can be a problem that needs to be addressed immediately.

## OVERALL ITCHING, SEVERE ITCHINESS

When you are pregnant, you are likely to experience itchiness in your belly and back area as your skin stretches and grows to accommodate for the growing baby. However, if you are noticing that your entire body is extremely itchy, particularly in your palms and the soles of your feet, you should call your doctor.

## SYMPTOMS OF JAUNDICE

Any symptoms of jaundice need to be immediately addressed by your doctor. This can include: yellowed skin or eyes, dark urine, and pale stools. If you have any of these symptoms, you need to talk to your doctor immediately as they will want to have you admitted to the hospital for treatment. Jaundice is caused by an underactive or infected liver, and this needs to be addressed immediately.

## IF YOU FALL OR EXPERIENCE A TRAUMA TO YOUR BELLY

If at any time in your pregnancy you fall or experience some kind of trauma to your belly, such as it being hit by something, you need to visit your doctor. While your belly will be fairly resilient, it is still important that you doctor ensures nothing has impacted the baby in a bad way. You should call your doctor immediately after a fall or blow to your belly to get help.

## IF SOMETHING JUST "FEELS" EXTREMELY WRONG

Some women do not have an exact symptom of anything wrong, they simply feel extremely wrong. If you think something is not right with your body, baby, or pregnancy overall, you should talk to your doctor. They will look over your vital signs and ensure everything is wrong. While in many instances this can arise from anxiety, in some cases this feeling can indicate something is wrong, despite no symptoms really being present. Always trust your intuition!

More Pregnancy Secrets No One Tells You

We hope that you have gained a lot of information that you did not already know about your pregnancy and are now preparing adequately. Pregnancy is an amazing journey, and, when you know everything that is probably going to happen, it can be an even easier journey for you to make. However, we are still not done and there are a lot of other pregnancy secrets that no one ever seems to tell you but you still must know. If you want to know the rest of those secrets, keep reading.

Touchy Feely Kind of World

It is up to you as to how you will react, but go ahead and start planning it now: People are going to touch your belly. Yes, you can expect all of your family and your friends to do it, and that is annoying enough. (If you don't think so now, just wait. You soon will understand.) But what is really, really bone chilling is that it is not just family and friends who will want to touch the baby belly. The ladies in the supermarket will simply need to put their hands on the belly. Every kid that you encounter when you are shopping is going to touch your belly, or at least ask if they can. Heck, even the mailman might see the belly and feel the desire to touch it. People come out of nowhere to touch a pregnant belly and they could care less to whom that belly is attached. It is just something about that pregnancy belly that people find irresistible. You can politely ask people not to do it, but if you are like most moms you will just suck it up and go with it. It's kind of nice to be fussed about after all.

## People Love to Talk

These is really no way to know what will come out of the mouths of some people upon learning that you are pregnant, so do not let anything that you hear surprise you. Sometimes, it is information that is very much unwanted, but it is all given to you with the best of intentions, in most cases. Be prepared for people to tell you things that you should be doing differently, giving you stories of how they did things and so much more. It is just a part of being pregnant, and yet another one of those things that everyone goes through while she is with child. Being prepared to hear some pretty off-the-wall statements can make dealing with them easier.

You will also want to prepare to be called "Mom" or "Mommy" by everyone. Kids love to do this, but adults are also in on it, too. This one isn't so bad, but it might come as a shock to hear it from some people, if you are not at least prepared to hear it.

It is kind of nice to be called a mom, but the real treat comes when your baby says it the first time!

## Stretch Marks

You have probably been waiting to see those two words this whole guide, wondering why you have yet to see any mention. But do not worry. We haven't forgotten them. We still look at them every single day so there is always that constant reminder there, even if we wanted to forget. People will tell you a lot about stretch marks. Every person has a different tale to tell: how to prevent them or how lucky she was not to get them. It is true that not all pregnant women get stretch marks, but for most women it is impossible to prevent them. If you are one of the lucky people for whom this is not an issue, you can thank your lucky stars for that. Stretch marks occur on the stomach, the arms and the legs, and oftentimes on the beasts, too. They occur due to the increase in the size, which stretches the skin, in such a short period of time. Stretch marks are often nice to see and they have a blue, red or purplish color. African American and Hispanic woman, as well as those of other dark skinned tones, are more likely to develop stretch marks and they are usually darker and deeper on these skin tones. There is not a lot that you can do about stretch marks. Watching what you eat so you do not gain a ton of extra weight is one step. Investing in a good cocoa butter lotion and using it on a regular basis can also help.

What's That Smell?

Have you ever wondered what it is like to be a drug-sniffing dog that has such a heightened sense of smell it can detect the faintest whiff of something? Well, we haven't either, but that is pretty much what it is like to be pregnant. You can smell everything and it is really intense. Many times you will find yourself asking, "What's that smell?" only to have other people tell you that they smell nothing. That is impossible, you think, because you can smell it so well. Your dog-like sense of smell is likely to develop at the very beginning of your pregnancy and continue until you have the baby. Sometimes it is a good thing and sometimes it is not, because you smell it all -- good and bad! Be prepared to have a Wonder Woman sense of smell.

The Movements Are Incredible

The first time that you feel your baby kick is an incredible feeling. It is incredible to feel all of his tiny little flutters and movements. Some people feel them earlier than others, but if you are paying close attention, you will be able to feel them quickly. Be sure that you have your journal ready to write all of these special feelings down.

Document Everything

This is probably not something that you will have any trouble doing. Most pregnant women love to take photos of their baby belly and their pregnancy, but many fail to keep a journal to document those special occasions. Do not assume that you are going to remember everything because you are not. Believe us, Mommy, you have yet to learn. There are tons of themed pregnancy journals and keepsake baby books that let you jot down those special memories and you very well should take advantage and use them. Remembering how you felt that first time you heard the sounds of that tiny heartbeat, how in love you were the moment that you found out, the first ultrasound and glimpse of your baby. These are all things that you want to document, but don't forget those other little and unexpected things. They are just as memorable and certainly a blast to look back upon later in life.  Snap pictures until your snapping finger hurts, and keep everything special that happens to you documented in that special journal. You will be glad that you did this later in life.

"I Want It and I Want It NOW"

Ordinarily in life, we see something that we want and we get it when we can. Yes, some things we want more than we want other things, but nonetheless we understand and do what we can to work on getting those items. But when you are pregnant, you will have cravings that are so intense that not getting what you want at that very moment is enough to send you into a tear-filled frenzy for hours on end. The cravings of pregnant women are immense, and sometimes they are also very odd. The body craves what it is lacking in most cases, so if you are eating healthy you are less likely to have those cravings. For most women, though, there will be something that you simply cannot live without and would drive 500 miles to get it. Expect this.

Hemorrhoids

Yep, the real pain in the butt. Hemorrhoids are for old people who aren't eating their Raisin Bran. That notion is incorrect. Anyone can get a hemorrhoid at any age, and when you are pregnant the odds of its happening are even greater. It doesn't matter if you're 20 or 40; pregnancy doubles the risk of hemorrhoids. Again, it is all about the added pressure on the body, the rectal area and the weight of the uterus. Hemorrhoids really hurt, and that pain intensifies while you are pregnant. You may or may not get a hemorrhoid, but it is important to know it is possible. If you have a hemorrhoid, it is difficult to go to the bathroom and it also makes it difficult to sit, lie down or do much of anything else. There are many over-the-counter treatments for hemorrhoids, should you be one of the unlucky ones who develop them. You can also talk to your doctor about treatment options, if you are getting them on a frequent basis, if the over-the-counter products are not working or if you are simply concerned with baby's health and want the expert advice first. You can also help lower the odds of getting a hemorrhoid by eating a well-balanced diet. It isn't just the Raisin Bran that can help with a hemorrhoid; many fruits and vegetables are high in fiber content.

Four Weeks & a Wake-Up

The last month of pregnancy is definitely the hardest. While the last trimester itself is uneasy, it is those last four weeks that seem to make even the calmest, gentlest of people feel as if are going to lose their minds. Prepare to be uneasy all of the time and probably really grumpy and biting the heads off of everyone who so much as speaks to you. Emotions and mood swings are also going to be really high. Remember, all of those hormones are going crazy inside of your body! Everything is going to make you cry, and there may be people who are looking at you with a lot of wonder in their eyes. Ignore them. If they are mothers, they will understand. The last four weeks also seem like an eternity, so expect that to be something that you experience as well. Soon you will be free, but in the meantime prepare yourself and everyone around you for this last month. Once they have been warned, all is fair in pregnancy.

# Chapter 8: Your Diet And Nutrition

Diet and nutrition is key to healthy pregnancy, and often the best solution to your prenatal care. Diet is the sum of the food you eat to meet your nutritional requirements. Nutrition is how you consume and use food to nourish your body. These two go hand in hand. You need to eat a well-balanced diet to receive good nutrition your body needs for healthy pregnancy.

Healthy Diet to Meet Nutritional Needs

Nutritional needs and requirements vary depending on a number of factors such as age, gender, weight, health condition, and whether one is pregnant or not. Being pregnant, you have specific nutritional needs and requirements you should satisfy to keep your body and the life inside your body healthy. The best way to give your body good nutrition is to eat a well-balanced diet.

Earlier, you already have an idea of how much weight you should add to help you and your baby grow safe and healthy the entire span of your pregnancy. This time, you will know why eating a healthy diet is necessary to your nutrition and how it can satisfy your nutritional requirements to make sure of your safe and healthy childbirth.

Your Nutritional Needs and Requirements

While nutritional needs and requirements may vary from one pregnant woman to another, here are some standards:

You need roughly 300 added calories day-to-day. This amount can go either up or down depending on your prenatal weight together with your activity level. If you happen to carry twins in your womb, the standard increases from 300 to 500 more calories daily.

While you measure the standard in terms of quantity or the number of calories, it is crucial that you also pay attention to the quality of your caloric intake, or the kind of food that you consume. You should get your calories from healthy or nutritious food.

- Increased amount of Vitamin D. You have to know that your baby is entirely dependent on your body to meet his/her need for Vitamin D. If you are not meeting your own need for this type of vitamin, you cannot expect your baby to meet his or her own, too. Lack of this vitamin has negative effects to the physical and intellectual development of your child.
- Extra Vitamin C of about ten (10) mg daily. Your blood carries Vitamin C to different parts in your body to your baby. During this travel, you may lose a certain amount. The standard recommended allowance is 80 to 85 mg. The limit is 1800 for 18 years and below, and 2000 for 19 years and above.
- What Vitamin C does is to protect your body and your baby from infection, to strengthen bones, to repair tissues, to stimulate mental development, and to help your body absorb an essential nutrient for pregnancy that is iron.
- Folic acid or folate to prevent your unborn to contract neural defects and cleft palate. It is best to supply your body with the right amount of folate before your pregnancy and or within the first two (2) months of your term. 200 to 400 mg each day during your trimester lowers the risks for neural tube defects (birth defects that affect the mental development and spinal cord of your baby).

- Riboflavin or Vitamin B2 of 0.3 mg more each day protects your baby from heart defects, and increase in Vitamin B12 of 0.2 mg daily will help your body cope with fetus development.

The recommended amount for other nutrients stays the same for both pregnant and non-pregnant women. It is important that you meet at least the minimum standard or requirement in your nutrition. This is to give your baby the healthy environment it needs for normal growth and development until he/she is born. Depriving your body of nutrients can result to birth defects and health problems, and can even endanger both lives, yours and your baby's.

What Makes a Healthy Prenatal Diet

Your diet is the primary source to satisfy your prenatal nutrition. You have to watch your diet more carefully for the growth and development of the life you carry in your womb. Eating a healthy and well-balanced diet is a must, especially for first time moms like you.

A well-balanced prenatal diet consists of the following:

- Carbohydrates, particularly the complex type, for energy you and your baby need. The Food and Drug Administration (FDA) suggests that you should get 55% of your daily calorie need from carbohydrates.
- Choose complex carbohydrates. The body uses them longer reducing fat build-up. What you get is more energy and healthier weight gain from its consumption. They are also a good source of fiber that can help you control unnecessary food cravings.
- Protein is extremely important, as it is the nutrient that builds the foundation of good health. You should give your body about 60-70 grams of protein daily while

pregnant or 15-25 gram increase from the usual daily nutrient recommendation.

The building block of cell development, protein and its amino acids are the primary nutrients responsible for fetus growth and development. Lack of it will result to several health issues and birth defects, most of which are life-endangering.

- Dietary fiber dramatically reduces the risks for health complications during your pregnancy. This is because fiber cleanses your body to flush out toxic substances. These substances are major contributors of health issues such as gestational diabetes.
- Fiber comes in two types, soluble and insoluble. Both are necessary, as each has its own specific benefits. Soluble fiber helps prevent gestational diabetes while insoluble fiber aids the digestive system and prevents constipation. Fiber will enable you to sustain healthy weight the entire course of your pregnancy.
- Vitamins and minerals are essential nutrients to keep you and your baby healthy. Remember that your baby is dependent upon you for his/her growth and development inside your womb. Essential vitamins and minerals protect the good health of your body and stimulate the best growth and development of your baby.

Certain types of food are rich in vitamins and minerals you need, such as fruits and vegetables. Natural food types are definitely better than processed food as sources of nutrients. In fact, health experts recommend natural over processed or instant food especially during pregnancy so your body receives the most nutrients you can get naturally from food.

- Water is the best way to hydrate your body, and hydration is a critical element during pregnancy. You lose more water in your body with frequent urination and perspiration while conceiving your child. You therefore need to increase your intake of water to replace what you have lost.

When your body becomes dehydrated due to lack of water, you may suffer from infection affecting the life inside you. Dehydration can also induce you to labor prematurely. To prevent unnecessary risks and complications, hydrate your body by drinking plenty of water. When it comes to drinking water, there can never be too much.

Food to Eat While Pregnant

During your pregnancy, certain food types can bring you the most benefits to improve your health and to make sure of the right nourishment for your baby. It is always best to choose food that has the most nutrients that can keep your healthy weight. Remember you need to add just the right amount of weight while you are pregnant.

The top ten foods when it comes to combined nutrients they have are the following (in no particular order):

- Asparagus is rich in fiber, folic acid, and iron, three of the most important nutrients your body should receive during pregnancy.
- Soy has vegetable protein, choline, fiber, folic acid, iron, potassium, and zinc.
- Legumes and beans are rich sources of vegetable protein, fiber, folate, iron, potassium, and zinc.
- Quinoa is a healthy seed that has lots of protein, folate, iron, and potassium.

- Milk has loads of essential vitamins and minerals like Vitamin D, B2, B12, calcium, and protein.
- Eggs are good sources of protein, choline, Vitamin B12, and selenium.
- Berries will supply your body with Vitamin C, fiber, folic acid, and they are also wealthy sources of antioxidants to protect your body from free radicals.
- Avocados are good sources of essential fats, choline, fiber, iron, potassium, and zinc.
- Salmon contains Omega 3 fatty acids, protein, Vitamin B12, and DHA or Docosahexaenoic acid, an essential fatty acid crucial to brain development.
- Yogurt has probiotic as well as Vitamin B12, calcium, and potassium.

The top ten food rich in folate or folic acid are the following (in no particular order and other than those mentioned above):

- Green leafy vegetables such as spinach. You can eat them as side dish or one of the main courses to for a well-balanced diet.
- Citrus fruits such as oranges. You can eat the fresh fruit for snack, extract the juice for refreshing beverage, or use it as an ingredient in preparing your healthy meal.
- Broccoli gives you about 24% of folate you need. It is also a savory way to detoxify your body naturally and safely during pregnancy.
- Lentils have high-density folic acid. Eating half a cup of lentils can satisfy 50% of your folate need.
- Sunflower seeds are versatile way to add folate to your diet. You can eat a handful as is as your snack, sprinkle it on your vegetable or fruit salad, and use it as an ingredient for baking. To get the most benefit, choose the unsalted variant.

- Tomatoes are also rich in folate. You can eat it raw, drink its juice, or use it as main ingredient such as with tomato soup.
- Okra is slimy but it is one vegetable loaded with folate. You can get about 37mcg of folic acid from a cup of cooked (preferably boiled or streamed) okra.
- Celery can give you 34 mcg of folate per cup. It is preferable to eat this vegetable raw or as ingredient to your fresh vegetable salad.
- Carrots are a delicious source of folic acid. It is also one of the most versatile sources to meet your daily nutrient need.

Whole grains and fortified cereals are folate boosters. Pair them with other folate sources such as broccoli, sunflower seeds, tomato juice, and others, you will experience dramatic increase in folate to satisfy your daily nutritional need.

The top ten food rich in iron (in no particular order) are the following:

Spinach is a super food that does not only contain loads of iron but other pregnancy nutrients as well. You can get about 3.2 mg of iron eating just half a cup of this super food.

Beef is a good source of iron, but choose lean beef meat for healthier way to get your nutrient. Each serving of beef meat can give you up to 3 mg of iron.

Each potato can give you 2.7 mg of iron. It is also a good source of your dietary fiber.

White beans have the highest concentration of iron among beans. It can easily give you 3.9 mg of iron per half cup.

Fortified cereals can start your day supplying your body anywhere between 2 mg to 21 mg of iron per bowl. What is best about these cereals is they are also rich in calcium and folic acid.

Prunes can satisfy both your iron and fiber needs. You can choose to eat the dried fruit or drink the juice; they both give you the same iron content.

Seaweed is rich in iron and a safe way to get Omega 3 fatty acids. It is also a good alternative to fish oils necessary for mental development of your baby.

Pumpkin seeds can really pump up your iron supply. You can eat its roasted seeds as snack, or include it as a recipe ingredient for texture and taste.

Clam chowder can give you about 23 mg of iron per bowl. Use tomato as soup base and you double the benefits, since the Vitamin C in tomato will allow your body to absorb the iron better. Tomato is also a good source of folic acid.

Liver pâté is very rich in iron. Chicken liver has high concentration of iron followed by beef liver. If you want to get the highest iron content, choose goose liver for your pâté recipe. Prepare just enough for immediate consumption as refrigerating it can expose the pâté to bacteria.

Food You Should Refrain from Eating

If certain food types help you satisfy your nutritional needs, there are those you should avoid while you are pregnant. The American Pregnancy Association lists the food as follows:

Uncooked seafood like oysters and raw meat from pork, beef, and poultry. Eating them puts you and your baby at risk for disease-causing bacteria such as salmonella. It can also cause food poisoning, which of course endangers your lives.

Fish with concentrated levels of mercury such as swordfish, shark, king mackerel among others. You can eat canned tuna but be very conservative in eating it. As much as possible avoid eating sushi or raw fish meat. To satisfy your Omega 3 fatty acid needs, you can choose to take natural dietary supplements such as fish oil. Consult your physician before taking any supplements.

Uncooked eggs to avoid the risk of salmonella. Be sure to check the ingredients as some readily available food such as mayonnaise, dressings, ice creams, or certain types of sauces and dips may use raw eggs. This is especially true for homemade recipes.

Soft types of cheese unless they only have pasteurized milk as ingredient can put you at risk for miscarriage. Similarly refrain from drinking unpasteurized milk as like soft cheese, it has Listeria, bacteria that can travel in your body to your baby and cause blood poisoning.

Caffeinated beverages can trigger miscarriages, low birth weight of your baby, and or premature childbirth. Caffeine works as a diuretic to rid of body fluids. It can result to dehydration and nutrient loss. Beverages that contain caffeine are coffee, tea, or sodas. Drink plenty of water instead. To add flavor and taste to water, you can choose to drink milk, fresh fruit or vegetable juices. You should remember though that they are not substitutes for your water necessity.

Avoid alcohol at all costs. Even the smallest amount of alcohol can already interfere with how the life inside your womb develops. It can cause serious harmful effects to your baby. Before, during, and after your pregnancy especially if you are to breastfeed your baby, you should refrain from drinking alcoholic beverages.

Unwashed fruits and vegetables. Especially with vegetables, they may contain traces of pesticides or toxic substances from the soil. It is also best to choose organic vegetables or homegrown fruits, as they are safer and has higher concentration of nutrients.

Natural Dietary Supplements

You may not meet your nutritional needs from your healthy diet alone. This is especially true for women who are not used to eating nutritious food before getting pregnant. To increase guarantee of giving the body essential nutrients, it is crucial to take dietary supplements.

However, you must exercise extreme caution and care in choosing your supplements. It is best to pick all natural food supplements that come from reliable and trustworthy manufacturers. You should also see to it to consult your physician before you take any supplements regardless of how safe they are.

Food Supplements Safe for Pregnancy

Several natural dietary supplements are available in the market. While they all claim to deliver safe results even for pregnancy, not all can bring health benefits. A few of these supplements, however, are necessary and important, some can do more harm than good, and the rests have no use at all.

Four (4) natural food supplements that are safe to take during pregnancy are the following:

Prenatal multivitamins - this is typically what physicians prescribed or recommend to their pregnant patients. It supplies the body with a combination of essential vitamins and minerals necessary for pregnancy such as iron, Vitamin B complex and D, calcium, and there are brands that have a substantial amount of folic acid as well.

Folic acid or folate - when you prenatal multivitamin does not include folate or folic acid, you can get it separately. Folic acid prevents birth defects. To maximize benefits from this nutrient, you should consume the food supplements before your pregnancy and or during the first trimester, and from then on increase the dosage up to the recommended limit.

Fiber dietary supplements are typically safe for use by pregnant women. These natural supplements help regulate hormones in the body that fluctuate during pregnancy. Fiber improves food digestion and prevents constipation. It is important that you drink a lot of water while taking dietary fiber supplements.

Fish oil food supplements are good sources of Omega 3 fatty acids. This is particularly useful to avoid harmful mercury in most fish meats. The supplements supply the body with essential fatty acids without the risks of exposure to mercury. Stay away from cod liver oil, though, as the amount of Vitamin A it has can bring adverse effects to your baby.

In choosing your food supplements, exercise extra care and caution. This is the time when being meticulous has the most benefit. See to it that you read the label and get all pertinent information about the product. Limit your choice only to those products that come from trusted brands and manufacturers. Ingredients must be all natural or organic and only the finest.

Most importantly, make sure that you consult with your physician before taking any of these food supplements. You can get recommendations from your physician and or discuss your options in taking dietary supplements to boost the meeting of or satisfaction of your nutritional needs. While food is the primary source of nutrients, supplements can fill in the gap to increase assurance that you are meeting your recommended daily intake of nutrients for your pregnancy.

What You Can Benefit from Food Supplements

The right choice of dietary supplements can bring several benefits to your pregnancy. They are the secondary sources of nutrients. Your healthy diet may not meet your specific nutritional needs. This is where supplements come in handy as they fill in the gap.

You have to keep in mind that the life inside your womb is completely dependent on your body for nourishment. When you eat, you do not just think about your own needs but also the nutritional needs of the baby you are carrying. Any nutritional deficiency on your body can take its toil on your baby.

It is also quite tedious to source all your nutrients from food. You will have to really plan hard and well and eat a lot to meet your needs. The least you would want is unnecessary stress and pressure as they are unhealthy for your baby. Dictary supplements help your body receive nutrients it needs without added calories from food.

Natural food supplements ease the burden of satisfying your nutritional needs. It does not mean, however, that you will depend your needs heavily on these supplements since they bring convenient results. As much as you can, you must source your essential nutrients from your healthy diet, as this is the best method you and your baby can benefit from your nutrition. Supplements should come in only as a gap filler. Some nutrients are difficult to source from food owing to your delicate condition.

Improve your dietary habits and start paying attention to the quality your food intake. Choose those that are highly nutritious, those that are rich in nutrients specific to healthy pregnancy but low in calories. Strive hard to meet your daily nutritional needs from food and fill in the gap by taking the right supplements. This is the best way to nourish your body so you and your baby get the most benefits.

# Chapter 9: Your Diet And Common Health Issues

Do you know that your diet plays a major role in treating and resolving common health issues during pregnancy? Often, it is the best and only solution you need to get well from health problems and ailments during your maternity period.

Natural Remedies for Morning Sickness

Morning sickness, or joint bouts of nausea and vomiting, is a popular symptom of pregnancy. Most pregnant women experience this symptom usually during the first three months. For some women, morning sickness can last the entire trimester and occurs not only in the mornings but also throughout the day.

To deal with this symptom effectively, you have to understand what triggers it. The main culprit for morning sickness is the fluctuation of your hormones, specifically the rise of your beta HCG or what you call as your pregnancy hormone.

Typically, nausea and vomiting is self-limiting. For pregnant women, this symptom goes away after the first trimester. Certain studies show that morning sickness is a mechanism of the body to protect you and your baby from the harmful effects of toxic substances.

With morning sickness comes your aversion for certain food. Amazingly, food items that you learn to hate are the types that have the most harmful chemicals. To relieve yourself of the symptom, a good natural remedy is to eat dry crackers or cereals. They are also rich in fiber and iron, two of the nutrients pregnant women need.

It also helps to limit your food intake to smaller portions but increase its frequency. You have to make sure that you are meeting your recommended nutrition with the amount and quality of food you eat. To prevent nausea and vomiting, drink your water at least half an hour before meals. You can also choose to drink it half an hour after meals. Drink plenty of water in between meals to hydrate your body.

It is best to stay away from spices and oily food. Choose to eat food that has less odor, as the smell can trigger you to feel nauseous and vomit. Ask your spouse or anyone in the family to take over the cooking chores, at least during the first trimester of your pregnancy. Give your body enough sleep.

Skin-Friendly Diet

Skin disorders and irritations are common to pregnant women, but these are the types that normally disappear after childbirth. If you want to keep your skin healthy, here is what food to eat and what food to avoid.

What Food to Eat

Here are at least five (5) food you should that serves as good nourishment for your skin. They contain nutrients to protect your skin from hormonal fluctuations to prevent or relieve skin irritations and disorders.

Avocado is rich in Vitamin E and antioxidants to protect your skin cells against damages from free radicals. This fruit has glutathione to help lighten the skin from hyper-pigmentation and keep it younger-looking.

Sweet potatoes are a power-packed source of nutrients containing Vitamins A, C, and E beneficial to the skin. You will benefit from the beta-carotene content of this food to prevent aging of the skin, specifically to delay wrinkles from showing.

Tomatoes have wealth of Vitamin C that builds collagen (protein necessary for tissue connection and support). It is also a good source of Lycopene, a substance that protects the skin from sun damage.

Walnuts keep the skin smooth and supple because of its alpha linolenic acid content. This nut is also a good source of beta-carotene and Vitamin E, and a delicious way to enjoy the healing properties of zinc.

Olive oil protects outer skin and prevents injury. It has the healthy fats the body needs and is one of the richest sources of Vitamin E, beta-carotene, and polyphenols that protect the skin from free radicals.


What Food to Avoid

If certain food brings loads of skin benefits, there are also those that are unfriendly and can worsen your skin problems. You should refrain from eating these food types.

Sweets and other food that has excess sugar are not only villains to your weight, but they can also worsen your pre-existing skin condition such as acne or fungal infection. What is more, sweets can speed up the aging of your skin to make you look older than your age.

Alcohol is a diuretic that can dehydrate your body and show on your skin. It is one food that is a completely no-no for pregnant women. It can heighten your skin problems and trigger other health issues putting you and your baby at higher health risks.

Processed and instant food contains chemical ingredients that can further disturb your already fluctuating hormones. Prevent toxic substances to enter your body and wreak havoc by avoiding this food type.


Gestational Diabetes Diet

Gestational diabetes is a health condition specific to pregnant women and easily controllable with the right diet. It is a common ailment during pregnancy where blood sugar level rises. If you fail to manage the condition, it can have serious effects on your baby.

One of the best natural ways to manage the condition is to watch your diet. Among the food groups that have dramatic influence on gestation diabetes is carbohydrates. But you cannot abstain from eating carbohydrates without disrupting your nutritional balance.

What you can do is to shift from eating food with simple carbohydrates to those that have complex carbohydrates and strictly follow a well-balanced diet. The difference between the two types of carbohydrates is their sugar content.

Simple carbohydrates have only one or two molecules of sugar that make it the fastest to digest and absorb. Unfortunately, it is also the type that has little nutritional value except rich calories. Examples of food containing simple carbohydrates are sugar, syrups, jams, jellies, soft drinks, and candies.

In contrast, complex carbohydrates have more sugar molecules that enable the body to use it longer. Since it is slow to digest, it does not mix with the blood easily. It is the type of carbohydrates that can keep your glucose or blood sugar stable. They also contain fiber that can rid your body of toxic substances and wastes efficiently. Examples are whole grains, green vegetables, beans and peas, potatoes and sweet potatoes, pumpkin, and corn.

Since your body needs energy from carbohydrates, it is best to source your energy from eating food that has complex carbohydrates. Make sure to eat just the right amount necessary to keep your diet well balanced. It also helps to supplement your diet with essential vitamins and minerals to meet your nutritional needs. Choose natural over processed food.

Strictly follow the recommended daily dietary allowance for pregnant women. Your primary source of nutrients should come from your healthy diet. Use supplements to fill nutritional gaps. Monitor your blood sugar level all throughout your pregnancy, and consult your physician regularly.

When you satisfy the nutritional needs of your body, you are activating and strengthening its own natural mechanism to protect and prevent any health issues, problems, and or diseases. Pregnancy is a delicate condition. It is wise to use natural remedies as they work with your body and not against it. However, you should always consult your physician for any remedy you wish to apply regardless if how safe it is. Getting the best of both worlds will definitely increase guarantee of safe pregnancy especially that this is your first time.

# Chapter 10: Labor And Delivery

Labor and delivery carries its own set of signs and symptoms, and things you should look out for. Unlike the three trimesters of your pregnancy, these symptoms are not going to last you very long, maybe a few hours to a few days at most. Some women may experience early labor symptoms for up to a week before labor starts, but these will generally be low in intensity until they get closer to active labor.

In this chapter, we are going to explore the signs and symptoms that labor is on the way. You will also learn about some of the basic things that you should expect in the delivery room, and how you can prepare yourself for the experience.

SIGNS OF LABOR

The following symptoms are signs that labor is preparing to start. These symptoms are generally felt at some point between 37-40 weeks, if you carry your pregnancy all the way to term. However, you may experience these symptoms earlier than that if you are going into preterm labor. If you start experiencing any of these symptoms, especially before 37 weeks, you should consult your doctor. They will tell you what to do, and when you should come in!

YOUR BABY "DROPS" INTO POSITION

Before labor starts, your baby will "drop" into position. You can tell this has happened when your baby bump is sitting lower down, and is more directed towards your pelvis. This is because the baby has officially prepared to enter the birth canal, so they are getting lined up and ready to make an appearance!

## YOUR CERVIX DILATES

Probably the most well-known symptom of labor starting is the cervix dilating. Of course, you probably can't tell this is happening, but your doctor will be able to tell you. In the days leading up to your labor, your cervix will begin to slowly dilate. Most women sit around 1-2cm for about a week or two before labor actually begins. Once labor starts, they will continue opening until they reach 10cm, which is when active labor starts.

## INCREASED CRAMPING AND LOWER BACK PAIN

You may notice more pain in your lower back and more cramping in your abdomen. This occurs as a result of your muscles preparing to put in all of the work to release your baby. This can also happen because the new position of your baby results in there being new pressures on your lower back and pelvic area. As well, your pelvis will be opening up the last little amount to let your baby come out, so your bones are quite literally stretching open.

## LOOSER JOINTS

The increased progesterone in your system are still responsible for your joints being loose, though you may notice this even more towards labor. You may experience popping or cracking in your joints a lot more, particularly when you move out of a position you've been sitting in for the same amount of time for a while.

## DIARRHEA

Many women experience diarrhea leading up to labor. This can be a displeasing opposite of the constipation that many women experience in the weeks beforehand. If you experience this, it's just because your muscles are loosening which means so are your bowel movements. Make sure you drink plenty of water, and prepare for labor to start!

## YOUR WEIGHT GAIN SLOWS DOWN, OR YOU LOSE SOME WEIGHT

Once your baby is fully "cooked" they will pretty much stop putting on weight, because they are getting ready to come out! So, if you notice you've stopped putting on pounds, or even if you lose a couple, this is why!

## YOU FEEL MORE FATIGUED THAN NORMAL

Because of your super-sized belly and all of your hormones, and the frequent need to urinate, it can be hard to get a full nights' rest. Because of this, you may find that you are consistently tired. The best thing you can do is sleep on the side closest to the washroom, and keep several pillows on hand to make those few hours of shut eye as restful as possible. As well, rest as much during the day as you can.

## YOU START NESTING

This is a common symptom of labor that you see often in the media on television shows and in movies. Nesting is a symptom many pregnant women experience towards the end of pregnancy as a means to prepare their home for the baby. If you find you suddenly have a burst of energy and all you want to do is clean and get everything ready for baby to come, it could be because baby is coming very soon!

## YOUR VAGINAL DISCHARGE CHANGES

Changes in vaginal discharge can include increased or thickened discharge, and a change in color. This is completely normal.

## YOUR CONTRACTIONS BECOME STRONGER AND MORE REGULAR

As your Braxton Hicks contractions change to actual contractions, you may notice they become a lot stronger and more regular in frequency. This is your body preparing to contract the baby out, and unless they are happening minutes apart for a long period of time, it is completely normal.

## BLOODY SHOW/MUCUS PLUG

As well as your vaginal discharge changing, you may experience your bloody show at some point. This happens as your mucus plug starts to fall out. You may notice a snot-like consistency that is streaked with blood. This is your mucus plug, and you don't need to worry about this, unless it's coming out before 37 weeks! Either way, you should tell this to your doctor just so they can be prepared for your impending labor!

## YOUR WATER BREAKS

The water breaking is one of the most famously known labor symptoms, but also happens to be one of the ones that happen the least! Only about 15% of women experience this symptom, and it's usually the last sign that labor is about to start. Make sure you let your doctor know as soon as your water breaks, especially if it breaks early.

## WHAT YOU SHOULD EXPECT IN THE DELIVERY ROOM

There are a lot of things to expect in the delivery room, and it varies based on how your pregnancy and labor have gone. If you are carrying a high-risk pregnancy, if you have a scheduled caesarean section, or if something goes wrong and your labor becomes an emergency caesarean section, you are going to have a totally different experience in the delivery room. In this chapter, we are going to only discuss what to expect in a healthy pregnancy where delivery occurs in a hospital room.

The delivery room is a scary and exciting place, and you may become overwhelmed with emotion while you are there. You are going to be going through a lot physically, and mentally. You are preparing to meet the life you've been creating for the past nine months, and that is a lot to take in! You are likely going to get hooked up to a no-stress-test machine that will make sure your fetal movements are strong and healthy, and to measure your contractions. You are also going to get your cervix checked on a fairly regular basis, to see how far you are progressing.

A good portion of your stay is going to be spent relaxing as much as possible so that you have the energy to get through the contractions. You may wish to spend some time in the shower or on a birthing ball, to help take some of the pressure and pain off of your abdomen. If it gets really hard, you may opt for pain medicines, such as laughing gas, or an epidural. If you were GBS positive, you will also be hooked up to an IV to get antibiotics every four hours.

Once labor begins, your doctor and a few nurses will come into the room. They will help coach you through pushing, and make sure your baby comes out safely. Your doctor may use forceps or a vacuum extractor to help take out your baby, if he or she needs a little assistance on the way out. Once your baby is out, your doctor will clamp the umbilical cord and let your partner cut the cord, if you have a partner involved. Then, you will be given a chance to have skin-to-skin contact with your baby, and nurse him or her. Sometime after your baby has been born, you will also have to push out your placenta, which is not a painful experience for most women, and takes minimal effort. The placenta is a tissue, so it will not stretch out your vagina as it exits your body, meaning you will likely not find it to be as painful, or painful at all.

Shortly after your baby is born, the nurses will take him or her for a few minutes to weigh your baby, and take some important measurements. You will then be able to shower off, and move into a more permanent room where you will remain for the rest of your hospital stay. About twenty-four hours after your baby is born, they will have their vitals taken to ensure that your baby is not suffering from jaundice or anything else. These are called heel-poke tests and they only take a few minutes for to do. Throughout the time you are there, your nurses will come in to check on you and your baby to ensure that you are both getting along well, and provide you with any support or assistance you may need along the way.

AN INSIGHT TO POSTPARTUM LIFE

The initial postpartum period is the hardest. You will be in "fourth trimester" until about six weeks after your baby is born. At this point, you are going to experience your postpartum bleeding, and many hormonal changes. Your body will be getting back into a balance from all of the pregnancy hormones, which can lead to many emotional and physical changes.

During these weeks, your baby is still going to have part of the umbilical cord - complete with the clamp - attached to their body. This will naturally fall off within' a few days once it dries up. Your baby may spit up a lot, which is completely normal as they are getting used to being able to digest food. Their poop is also weird, as it will be a blackish green color, or it could be yellow or brown. The color of newborn poop varies, and can also vary in texture. As long as it is not pale, you should be okay.

Getting to sleep through the night will be hard with your newborn, as they will want to eat frequently. Ideally, you should sleep during the day when your baby sleeps, at least for the first little while, as this will help you replenish the sleep you are losing through waking up all hours of the night. Having a strong support system in place is also helpful.

# Chapter 11: What to Expect - Labor Induction

Many women hear the topic of induction and they do not know exactly how to respond. The thought that your body does not want to go into labor on its own, or that your baby would be safer if they were delivered under a medical induction can be terrifying. However, if you take the time to understand the process, it will not be nearly as scary as it sounds.

What is Medical Labor Induction?

There are many medical reasons to have your labor induced. Your body naturally creates the hormones necessary to start your labor. However, some women do not create enough of the hormone to really get labor going strong enough to bring your baby into this world. Sometimes, your body just needs a little boost.

When your doctor has decided that it is time to induce your labor, he will give you an IV medication called pitocin. This will help start contractions and help to thin out your cervix.

Who Should Be Considered for Induction?

There are many reasons that your doctor may consider you for induction. These reasons are:

- gestational diabetes

- pre-eclampsia

- going past your due date (41 weeks pregnant)

- if the health of you and your baby are at risk by continuing the pregnancy

- ... and other medical conditions that affect you and baby

What about inducing for non-medical reasons?

Are you just tired of being pregnant? Or does your doctor have something planned during the time of your due date? Does this have you thinking about inducing early? Did you know that almost 25 percent of the inductions are not medically necessary or are elective according to the Center for Disease Control Moms and experts are hot on the topic of induced labor during non-medical reasons.

Inducing before 39 weeks have not been recommended by the American College of Obstetricians and Gynecologists. If you induce earlier than 39 weeks there is a risk of bringing a child into the world that is not fully developed. "Induction can carry risks that should only be used for medical reasons," says Sabine Droste, MD. She is a professor at the University of Wisconsin-Madison of obstetrics and gynecology.

There are certain situations where if the doctor thinks that they are close to deliver but live too far away or won't make the drive to the hospital the doctor may make a call to induce. This would keep a birth from happening on the road, or anywhere outside of the hospital.

What are the risks of non-medical induction?

There are times when family come to see the birth of your child or we are so busy that we would like to have the delivery at a certain time. This can cause for a treat amount of temptation to induce your pregnancy because of this. Other times people think and say that you are too big and you will have to have a C-section in order to have your child. This can scare mothers to try and induce labor before truly knowing if the baby really is too big or not.

You should really think about this and be cautious because you could complicate things. Just because you induce early does not mean you will not need to have a C-section. The chances of having a C-section are about as equal of a chance as the baby actually being too big to need a C-section. You should wait to make this decision after discussing with your doctor the options you have taken and thought about.

How is labor induced?

When there is a patient that has a cervix that is insufficiently dilated, the cervix needs to be softened. We do this by using prostaglandin which is a hormone. After the cervix is softened another hormone called oxytocin is administered to help trigger labor. Pitocin is usually intravenously administered. Inducing labor is much easier when there are already signs of labor early on. This is because the body is ready to go.

There are other ways of inducing labor, such as breaking the amniotic sac releasing the amniotic fluid. This is done by puncturing the amniotic sac with a sterile plastic like hook. When the amniotic fluid is released it contains prostaglandins. This will help to increase the frequency and strength of your contractions. If this does not induce labor than there is a larger risk that infection can spread to your baby because there are no fluids to protect the baby any more.

There is a different procedure called membrane sweeping. This involves breaking the membrane connections from the uterus. This is supposed to force the cervix to start dilating and effacing which should help to start contractions.

Although these are methods that are used, it does not mean that they will always work. It all depends on how the mothers body will react when these actions are taken. The mothers body can react differently to any of these. It could cause labor to run fast and smooth or it could make things take longer.

Do natural inducers really work?

Here are popular methods that are used. You can decide for yourself if they are effective.

Walking has been used to try and help move the baby into a position that uses gravity that can help.

Stimulating your nipples can help release oxytocin and can start contractions. Although doctors give caution to this method because it can also cause contractions that will last longer and cause distress to your baby.

The Pineapple fruit has a chemical in it called bromelain. This can help to soften the tissues connected to the cervix.

Sex can be a fun way of trying to speed things along. This is because semen has cervix-softening prostaglandins in it.

Spicy foods can also help kick the body into full gear and get your innards moving. But if it does not work it could just cause you to have gas.

# Chapter 12: What to Expect – Having a C-Section

There are so many women who have their birth plan in mind through their full pregnancy.

They have memorized and read about all the details. Many end up learning that the best chance for the safety of their child is for them to be delivered through C-section. This can be upsetting when this was not the plan they had in mind all this time. This change in plans can cause the feeling of fear, guild and dread causing them to tailspin. In all reality women should always keep in mind that things can and may happen to change how the delivery of their baby may go.

The C-section is no way any woman wants the birth to go but in certain situations it becomes necessary. Here we will discuss what you can expect if your doctor says the better way is to have a C-section. Sometimes the doctor may call that a C-section should be done because of certain complications that the doctor has noticed. Other times it happens during labor when the baby is not reacting well with the contractions you are having.

When a mother hears C-section mentioned it automatically causes fear to develop. We will discuss issues that are common with unplanned C-sections.

Typical Immediate Fears

C-sections are commonly talked about and how they are so awful. This can cause instant dread and questions to flood your mind. Some of these worries are would it ruin my experience of birth? Will there be an excruciating and long recovery time? Would I be left with big ugly scars?

Will this C-section be unnecessary?

The decision in performing a C-section is made by 2 physicians. They are quite common and happen in 1 out of 4 births. Some reasons that C-sections are taken into account are for multiple pregnancy, large baby, labor failure, diabetic medical conditions, fetal distress, placenta Previa or high blood pressure.

Will the Surgery Be Long and Scary?

It is normal for any major surgery to make you apprehensive. You will feel pressure and a slight tugging when they pull the baby out. It should be a painless procedure that takes around 45 minutes. The baby is usually born within 10 to 15 minutes from the start of the operation.

Most of the C-section is performed with the mother awake. To relieve pain, the mother can have a spinal block or epidural which will numb the lower portion of the body.

Epidurals are usually used in labor and it will be topped off before the surgery of a C-section. The Spinals are given when there is a scheduled cesarean. They last only about 1 or 2 hours and can be easily administered. They reserve general anesthesia in rare cases or emergencies when the spinal or epidural does not work.

The surgery starts with an incision above the bikini line into the abdomen wall. A second incision is made in the uterus wall where the delivery of the baby takes place. They then cut the umbilical cord and remove the placenta and close the incisions.

When the surgery is all done Duramorph is usually administered for a long-lasting pain reliever. This helps for any discomfort after the spinal or epidural has stopped working.

Will this rob me of the experience of giving birth?

It is not a regular birth but the mother is awake and will experience her baby being delivered into this world and into her arms.

You should not blame yourself for a C-section and that the planned labor did not go as was planned. As long as the baby is healthy and delivered than the birth was a success. You should be happy that you just brought a life into this world.

Will a C-section prevent me from bonding with my baby?

When you have a C-section you are awake to witness it and most times you will have your baby handed to you right after birth. This allows for you to hold your baby and love them.

Will recovery be extremely painful and difficult?

You are held for around 4 days at the hospital where you will experience pain around the areas where the incisions were made. It will also be difficult to get out of bed and back in bed unassisted. You will be given a couple of types of drugs to help manage pain. Percocet will most likely be prescribed as a painkiller. Sometimes a morphine drip that can be self-administered will be given so that the patient can press a button when the pain gets to be too much.

There are ways that you can help to lower the pain and increase the speed of recovery. Drinking warm water has been suggested. This can help you to pass gas. This shows that you can start eating solid foods again. It is also suggested that if you have had a C-section that you get out of bed the day after surgery or as soon as possible.

This helps to loosen up the muscles around the incision area and can get you back to wanting to get up and go.

Medication will help to ease the pain so that you can get out of bed and you shouldn't be afraid to use it.

When you get home keep getting up and moving but don't over work yourself and do strenuous work. You will begin to feel better in as little as a week.

Will I have a scary, ugly scar?

At first the area can be red. There will be a thin scar just above your pubic hairline. The incisions are usually 5 to 6 inches in length so that there is enough room for the shoulders and head of your baby to be delivered. Over time the color and size of your scar will face where only your husband, doctor and if you have one your bikini waxer will only see. You can also look at your scar as a happy remembrance of when you brought your child into this world.

Will all of my future babies have to be born through C-section?

Doctors for the longest time always stuck with the saying that once you had a C-section you would always have a C-section. This is no longer how it is looked at. There is now a 70% success rate of vaginal birth after cesarean and it is increasing as a safe option.

But as with any surgery there can always be more complications that can cause serious risk. You should always allow your doctor to consider and evaluate if it is an option for your next birth or not. Always make sure to consult your doctor and ask those important questions in moderation during your office visits.

# Chapter 13: Preparing for Delivery

New moms have a great training tool for delivery available. Classes are a good idea for any first time mom. There are different types of classes available to any new mama that she can take advantage of. A birthing class is a great choice, you can go alone or with your partner, and you will find most hospitals offer this for first time parents. Usually this is free of charge. That is helpful because as you know you are starting to spend a lot of money on the new baby! A birthing class will walk you through delivery step by step.

Truth time. You are probably going to see a movie showing someone actually giving birth. It may make you swoon in anticipation of your big day or it may make you want to vomit. If the latter feeling overtakes you do not worry. This is normal. When it is your body and your baby it suddenly will not seem icky in any way. If you take a class at the hospital you plan to deliver at that is great because they will take you on a tour of the hospital and birthing area. Now if you find out that you will be in a room with another mom during delivery do not despair. When you are in labor you will just plain not care. All you will be focused on is working through the contractions, controlling the pain, and preparing to meet your new bundle of joy. Of course, there will be a curtain separating the two laboring mothers so you will have privacy.

Birthing classes will also teach you the importance of how to breathe. You may have seen a movie where a mom gives birth. It may seem funny when the mom is "hee hee hoo hooing" however that type of breathing is most beneficial and really does help to control the pain!

After the baby is born you will either breastfeed or bottle-feed. The choice is yours. However, you do need to be aware that breastfeeding is extremely good for your child. Especially, the first few days when the colostrum is in your breasts before your milk lets down. There may be reasons you are unsure about breastfeeding. Do you have to go back to work? You can work and breastfeed. You can pump on your lunch and breastfeed before and after work and throughout the night. You can also choose to alternate bottle and breast. Breastfeed when you are home and let the baby drink formula when you are working. That is ok! Some breast milk will still give your baby all the necessary and helpful nutrients that she needs. There will be classes after the baby is born on breastfeeding. If you are having difficulty or not sure about breastfeeding then these classes would be helpful to you. Also, most if not all hospitals have lactation consultants and they will help you. Not to mention, they will definitely understand all the feelings you are having and work you through it.

Have you thought about the birth experience yet? There are several things you need to decide. Who do you want in the room with you when you are giving birth? Yes, you may want visitors during labor and that is different than giving birth. When you are ready to push the stirrups come out and privacy disappears. The choice of who to have in the room with you when you are bringing a child into this world is a very personal decision. You may only want your partner. You may want your partner and your mom. You might not care who is in there. The hospital usually only lets two people in the room at a time though. If you originally thought that you wanted perhaps your mom or his mom in the room and you change your mind that is ok. It is hard to let someone know that you no longer want anyone in the room. This is one of the times that you will be so happy to have your nurse around. Labor and delivery nurses have no bones about telling visitors that they cannot come in the room. In fact, they will probably lie for you and say it is their decision to avoid any hurt feelings. Remember though, this is your big day! Just like a wedding you get to make the decisions. If someone's feelings get hurt that is okay, they will get over it. When you are laboring to bring your child into this world it is up to you, and only you, who is there with you.

It is a good idea to have some sort of birth plan. First up, drugs. Do you plan on getting an epidural? Do you plan on delivering natural? You should have a general idea of what you want and do not be shy about speaking up. Truth time. You may change your mind. That is ok! If you planned on going completely natural and the pain is getting too intense for you then it is okay to get the epidural. Do not feel bad about this. You are not a wimp. You are a smart woman who is doing what is best for her and her child. On the other hand, you may be doing okay and decide to hold off on the epidural and end up going natural. If you are trying to go natural and at the last minute decide you want an epidural it may be too late. There is a point where it is about to be pushing time that the doctor will no longer allow the epidural to be administered.

Another thing to decide is do you want to walk around or lie down throughout the contractions. Again, you may very well change your mind. If the contractions start to slow down walking the halls of the maternity ward can help to speed it back up. Do you want music? Do you want to use an exercise ball to roll on? No matter what you decide make sure it is about making you as comfortable as possible during the labor and delivery experience.

# Chapter 14: What to Expect - Bringing Baby Home

No matter how many children you have, bringing every new baby home is a unique experience. No two babies are the same, which surprises many parents. This is especially the case when they bring home a new baby and their personality is the exact opposite of their previous children. The truth is, every child is different, and many of these differences are noticeable as soon as their baby comes into this world.

Ten Important Facts About Newborns

Let's face it, you never know exactly what to expect from a newborn, especially if you are a new parent. Here are ten important facts that you should know about newborns that no one else will tell you.

1.      Your baby may look, well, strange. Baby's heads typically appear squished for a few weeks. This is because they were repeatedly squished as they passed through the birth canal. Also, newborn's faces are typically puffy and a little swollen. Some babies may have bruises on the bonier places of their face too.

2.      Your baby won't reward you for at least the first six weeks. Every parent looks forward to hearing their new baby coo and smile. Unfortunately, baby's typically do not reach these milestones until they are about six weeks old. Don't worry, it is well worth the wait.

3.      Babies must have a sponge bath until their umbilical cord falls off. This usually takes about two weeks. The good news is that babies do not really get dirty at this age, so getting a few sponge baths will not cause hygiene problems.

4.     Your baby's soft spot is not as sensitive as you would think. It is just fine to brush his hair and touch his head. You may feel the soft spot pulsate when you touch it, but this is only because of the blood vessels surrounding the area.

5.     Your baby WILL let you know if she is getting enough food. Your baby should eat every two to three hours at first. However, if she is hungry more often, she will definitely let you know. Many pediatricians are slowly moving toward mothers feeding their baby's at will, rather than keeping them on a strict schedule. Over time, your baby will regulate her eating habits to a set schedule.

6.     Babies have dry skin and their isn't much you can do about it. Think about it like this. If you spent 9 months floating around in a pool and decided to get out, your skin would dry out over a few days too. While you do not technically have to do anything about it, you can apply some Johnson's pink baby lotion if it makes you feel better.

7.     You and baby are not hostages when you come home. You can come and go whenever you and baby please. The only thing you must ensure is that anyone who touches your baby must wash their hands first.

8.     Babies cry ALOT. This is how your baby communicates. These ear piercing screams will let you know that your baby is hungry, cold, has a messy diaper, or wants you to hold them. The only problem is that these early conversations can be extremely frustrating for both of you. Over time, you will learn what each wail means.

9.     Babies may sleep a lot, but they do not sleep for long stretches of time.  It is important that you wake your baby up every three hours to get changed and eat. Do not wake your baby up during the night, they will wake up if they need

something. By following this schedule, your baby will learn the difference between day and night schedules.

10.                    The first few weeks will be the most stressed, lonely and tired days of your life. These are the difficult times that prepare you for the rest of parenting. Rest assured, it will get better faster than you think.

Leaving the Hospital

Do not overdress your newborn baby for his or her 1st trip home.  If you think you will be too warm in a knitted cap during the day, think that the same will apply to your baby.  It is alright to dress your baby in a baby blanket over bare legs or a T-shirt and light cotton pants when the weather is warm. During cooler or cold days, you can wrap your baby in a hat, footsie pajamas and warm blanket.  But always check that the blanket is far from the face of your face to prevent him or her from being suffocated.  It is also important that you choose clothes simple clothes that do not need a lot of pulling and pushing of your newborn baby's legs and arms.  Before you leave the hospital, make sure that you have raised all your questions to your doctor so that you will have peace of mind when you get home.

During the Car Trip

The car seat is considered as the most essential thing you need during your baby's first trip home. All states require parents to ensure that their babies have a car seat before they leave the hospital.  You can opt to buy, rent or borrow a car seat even before your due date.  This will give you enough time to carefully inspect the car seat for safety.  You can choose between infant-only car seats or convertible car seats. If you decide on an infant-only car seat, make sure that you replace it when your baby grows to more than 22 to 35 lbs.  Many parents prefer a convertible car seat so that they will not need to buy a new one when their baby grows older.

First-Time Emotions

It is natural to have mixed emotions during your baby's first trip home. This is particularly true for first-time parents. There will be both nervousness and excitement. You may also feel sore and physically drained, depending on your experiences during labor and delivery. Your mixed emotions can also be the result of hormone imbalances caused by the childbirth.

You may also start to feel anxious as you think about the needs of not only of your newborn baby but the needs of your partner and other kids, as well. Even visits from family and friends can add to your stress level. Amidst all these emotions, it is very important that you talk to and seek help from your partner and other loved ones who are willing to help.

When to Call the Doctor

Pediatricians are used to first-time moms calling them often during the first few weeks after the baby is born. First-time moms, in particular, can worry too much even for the littlest things. If ever you come to a point when you are not sure whether to call your doctor or not, here are some signs that can tell to do so immediately:

1.   More than 8 diarrhea stools within eight hours.

2.   Rectal temperature is 38 degrees Celsius (100.4 degrees Fahrenheit) or higher. This is particularly important for babies younger than two months.

3.   Bloody stool or vomit

4. Symptoms of dehydration such as no wet diapers in six to eight hours, a depression in the soft spot on the head of the baby and sunken eyes.

5. Inability to keep fluids down or repeated forceful vomiting.

6. A soft spot that protrudes when your baby is upright and quiet.

7. Labored or rapid breathing. Immediately call 911 when you notice that your baby starts to turn bluish around the mouth or lips and has difficulty in breathing.

8. When your baby is difficult to rouse.

Always be aware of your new baby's condition. Even minor conditions can at times change rapidly for young babies.

# Chapter 15: Tips for First Time Moms

1. Prepare Your Mind

   Your Whole Life Will Change

So let me put it to you straight. Whether you planned your pregnancy or it "just happened", being a Mom will change your life. Your entire life. I'm sure you've heard this before, just as you're hearing it from me now. You probably won't totally understand it until you're holding your child in your arms and have taken care of him or her for the first few weeks. Still, I'll try to explain. Your life without children is free and your responsibilities are based on what you need and what needs to be done to maintain your life and needs. When you bring a child into your life, you still need to take care of yourself, yes. But your main priority is making sure your child has everything he or she needs and is safe. For example, in your life without a child, if you have some extra money or want to do something special for yourself you may go get your nails or hair done. With a child, there may not be extra money. Or if there is, you'll probably spend it on your little one instead of yourself. A mom usually does (and should) think about what her child needs before herself. You will start thinking this way when your child is born, but you should start rearranging the way you think now so it will be an easier transition.

Think About Who You Allow In Your Life

 Not only should you start to think differently about financial priorities, but about who you allow in your life, and now your child's life. Childless, you have only yourself to think about when choosing what relationships you allow in your life. When I say relationships, I mean romantic and otherwise. If you're single and pregnant, now is not the time to start a new romantic relationship. Now is the time to focus on being ready for your child. If you're already in a relationship with the baby's father (your boyfriend or husband), make sure that you have open communication with him about how you're going to parent your child together. Also, fix any problems you have in your relationship because your relationship problems will affect your child's life. If you have any friends or family who you know aren't good for you or are negative about the baby, keep them at a distance or let them know that you don't want any negativity in your life and around your child. Any close unhealthy relationships in your life can affect your child by causing him or her stress and can even delay development.

Don't Stress

Bringing a child into the world is going to change your life, yes, but don't stress yourself out! There will be less time for yourself. There is a whole other life to consider, yes. But you still need to take care of yourself. In order to be a good mom, you do need to make sure you're healthy too. Whatever stress you're dealing with will affect your child too. Being organized with your time will help to decrease stress. Taking time for yourself will also be important. Even a five minute break can center you and refocus your mind. You may find yourself hiding in the bathroom at some point in time to get a breather! Some good ways to destress are taking a walk (with or without your baby), sitting down and drinking a cup of hot tea, or reading a book for five or ten minutes.

2. Take Care Of Your Body

Take Care Of Yourself

Pregnancy takes your body through a lot. If you're planning to get pregnant, start getting your body in the best shape possible now. If you're already pregnant, you'll be limited in what exercises you can do, but still take care of yourself and do what you can do. Definitely ask your doctor what's safe. You want your body to be strong and prepared for the birth.

Exercise

Like I said, if you're already pregnant, there will be limited exercises you can do. Especially if you're a beginner exerciser. Moving your body and being fit will still be important. If you can do nothing else, walking is always a good option. Swimming is low impact and is good for pregnant women. It can be done at any stage of pregnancy. There are other options, but again, make sure you ask your doctor what's safe for you. Especially if you have health risks. After giving birth, the time to wait to begin exercise again is usually six weeks. You'll want to start doing safe exercises as soon as possible to get your body back into shape so that you can keep up with that little one! You may not have as much energy after delivery, and getting into an exercise routine will help your body get its strength back, as well as lose any extra baby weight. Of course, what you're putting into your body is important too...

Diet

Exercising to stay in shape is important, but it goes hand in hand with your diet. When you're a new mom, what you eat is more important. The importance of eating for energy becomes more evident. If you eat too much junk food, you will notice! Recovering from the pregnancy and delivery and at the same time, adjusting to having a new baby can take a toll on your body. You need to continue taking vitamins. Make sure that you make time to eat enough. And make what you do eat count! Include vegetables and leafy greens in your diet like broccoli, kale, spinach, and carrots. When you go shopping, check out the produce section and try new vegetables you haven't tried or didn't like before. Also, eat protein sources like chicken breast, eggs, Greek yogurt and beans. Calcium is one of the most important minerals for women to pay attention to, so drink milk and eat yogurt or cheese. If you don't eat dairy, try alternative calcium sources like soy milk, or take a calcium supplement. Finally, after grocery shopping, don't be afraid to try something new in the kitchen! When your little one grows into a toddler, you're going to need to try new dishes for his or her little taste buds anyway!

Pampering Yourself

As a mom, no one is going to take care of you more than you can take care of yourself. No, pampering yourself is not frivolous, either! It's important for your mental well being, as well as your physical well being. After all of that washing and sanitizing, put lotion on your hands. Wear a pretty scent you enjoy. Buy yourself a new nail polish. Light a candle and enjoy a few minutes of a book or drink some tea or coffee. Or wear some nice lacy underwear under your mom clothes. These are just a few examples of pampering yourself, but you can come up with some of your own, based off of what you enjoy.

3. Change Your Priorities

Getting Into A Routine

You're not number one anymore! This can take some getting used to. At the newborn stage of your child's life, you may feel like you don't even have time to take a shower some days. All of the appointments you need to keep, being up late hours of the night feeding, washing dirty baby clothes, preparing bottles, etc. Taking care of a newborn takes up most of your time. Getting into a routine will help you to stay sane as well as stay on track with everything that needs to be done. If you're lucky enough to have someone to help you the first few weeks, good for you. Not everyone does, but that can definitely be an advantage. As you're learning your baby, try to set the same time of day for washing and filling bottles, laundry, nap time and bed time.

Your New Obligations

Being that you have more to do on a daily basis, you may need to learn to say no and cut some things out of your life. Before you welcome your child into the world, it's easier to fit fun activities such as date nights and time with friends into your schedule, but with a child, especially a newborn, it's not so convenient. You'll be staying home with your child a lot. Finding a babysitter isn't always so easy. For the first few weeks, you should keep your baby home in order not to expose him or her to extra germs and sick people anyway. Also, there will probably be a lot of people who want to visit and see the new addition to your family. Let some of them know that you don't want visitors for the time being. You're just getting your family adjusted to having a new little one and don't need extra company to entertain.

Remember To Stay Positive

So you're giving your baby the majority of your time, and your body is healing at the same time. It's easy to be stressed with everything going on. Keep it in your mind that your baby is a blessing and a positive addition to your life! Being a mother is not an easy job, but it's rewarding and helps you see what's most important in life.

4. Get Ready To Change Your Schedule

Get A Planner Or Calendar

To be successful and to make the most out of your time as a mom, you need to have a good schedule. I strongly suggest having a planner or calendar where you plan what you're doing with your time and for taking notes. To make it fun, pick one that's cute and fits your personality. Even go and get hilighters to mark the most important points. If you choose a calendar, hang it in a place where you'll always see it. Write down every doctor appointment, mark down feeding times, family events you need to remember, even grocery lists and lists of household chores that need to be done. Your planner will be like a reference to keep track of your time.

Planning Ahead

Your schedule will be different if you're working than if you're a stay at home mom, but is important either way. Have a plan for your days from start to finish. Plan what time you'll get up. Make sure it's before you know your child will wake up so that you'll have time to shower, get dressed and get your focus. You'll have time to pray or meditate if that's a part of your life, and write look over your schedule to see what you have planned for the day. Also, it will be so much easier for you to shower and get dressed by yourself than when your little one is already awake and demanding your attention. Getting up earlier may be forfeiting a little sleep, but your day will go so much better.

Your Diaper Bag

A really important part of preparing for your days will be your diaper bag. Leaving the house with your baby unprepared can be very inconvenient. Keeping the diaper bag ready with everything in it, kept in the same spot can make things go smoother when you're getting ready to take baby out. Some essentials you'll need to keep in there will be diapers, baby wipes, an extra change of clothes, prepared bottles, a toy to keep your little one busy, snacks for an older baby or toddler, and a cloth to wipe any spit up.

5. Buying Baby Items

### Where Your Baby Will Sleep

One of your biggest purchases you'll make for your baby is going to be a crib. There are different options you have for where your baby will sleep. A lot of cribs nowadays are designed for the stages of life. The crib stage, when your baby is first born and through the first year. It will convert into a toddler bed when your baby is ready, then into a big kid bed. There's also the option of buying a bassinet for your newborn. It takes up less space, but can only be used for a few months, until your little one is too big for it. Something that you'll need, whether your baby sleeps in it or not, is a pack and play. A pack and play is a portable play pen that you can put your baby in during the day to play in and stay safe while you're busy and watching close by. This can also be where he or she sleeps. You can choose this option if you're trying to conserve space or for travel. It can be folded up when not in use and taken with you if you're spending the night somewhere besides home with baby. The choice is yours, just make sure that baby is safe wherever he or she is sleeping. It is not a good idea to have your baby sleep in bed with you.

### Diapers And Wipes

This will be your biggest expense! It's a good idea to stock up. If you're planning on having a baby shower, you'll probably get a lot if there are a good number of people coming. If you want to, instead of a baby shower, you can throw a diaper party. Just cook some food and invite friends and family over, asking them to bring diapers for the baby. It's not important to buy all one brand. What is important is that when you stock up or have people buy them, that different sizes are purchased. When baby comes, pay attention to how he or she reacts to the diapers. If your little one gets a rash from one brand of diapers, don't buy those ones anymore! Same goes for baby wipes. Your best bet is getting unscented baby wipes.

Bottles

Unless you're exclusively breast feeding and you're not storing milk (it's all coming straight from you to your baby), you're going to need to buy bottles. There are so many different brands and types of bottles, so I suggest that you go shopping and look around. See what your options are. The most important thing will be the nipple on the bottle and whether your baby is taking the milk from it. The same with a pacifier. If you buy different pacifiers, you'll soon know which one is your little one's favorite.

Clothes

When buying clothes for your baby, keep in mind how quickly your baby will grow. So you may not want to go out and buy the most expensive clothes you can find for your baby. I know you'll want to get some cute things for your little one. That's natural. So why not buy a special outfit for each holiday? If you have family members who have older kids and have left over baby clothes they won't use again, they may want to hand them down to you.

Car Seat And Stroller

With both a car seat and stroller, you have so many to choose from. Again, I suggest that you look at your options. Go online and research what's out there. Even go in the stores and see what they have. Choose which is right for you. Keep in mind that most hospitals will want to check that your car seat is safe before letting you take the baby home with it. You may want to ask to make sure.

Other Items

There are so many extra baby items out there on the market that you won't necessarily need but may want to consider A couple of them include baby bottle sanitizers and baby wipe warmers. Part of the fun of preparing for baby is shopping!

6. Your Support System

A good support system will be a big help to you when you have your baby. Knowing who to call and who to trust when you need someone to watch your child is valuable. It will help you to stay sane as a busy mother, and will be a benefit to your child. Your support system doesn't have to be huge either. If you get overwhelmed and need some rest or need to go somewhere important where you can't take your child with you, have at least one or two people you can call.

When you think of all of the people you know, you can come up with all of the people you know that you'd trust to watch your child. Whether it's your mom or dad, sister or brother, best friend, or your neighbor who you've known for years. Before the baby is even here, go to each one of the people you trust and want to be a part of your support system. Let them know that you would like them to be a part of your child's life. Ask them if they'd be available to watch your child at times. Find out what their schedules are. After the conversation you have with each person you want to be a part of your support system, if they are good fit to be a baby sitter, write their name, phone number and address in your planner.

Knowing who you're going to call when you need someone to watch your little one, and even who you're going to call when you need some new mother advice is another way to be prepared going into motherhood. If you go through your mental Rolodex and can't think of anyone you would trust with your child, find people! For support as a mother, there are so many different forums and support groups to be a part of where women come together and have created their own community. Google "mom support group forums online" and there are many places online that you'll find to be a solace to you. Another option you have if you'd rather meet people face to face is to join a group for mothers in your community. Ask your local hospital, church, or community center about groups there are for mothers in your area. A big plus is that usually, there will be childcare at a support group for mothers.

7. Welcoming Your Little One

The Hospital

After all of the preparation you've done changing your priorities, getting mentally and physically ready for baby and buying baby items, now comes the time to welcome your new baby into your home. First, lets talk about the hospital. Make sure that you bring the car seat to the hospital when you go in to deliver. Also, make sure that you pack a bag for yourself and the baby. Include a change of clothes for yourself and a robe. Put socks, clean underwear and a pair of slippers in your bag. Remember a camera for pictures. You'll want to capture those first moments of life. For the baby, pack an outfit for him or her to go home in. Also, bring a baby blanket. You won't need to bring diapers because the hospital with will supply you with them during your stay.

Your House

Before you go into labor, set up your baby's bedroom. Put the crib together. Set up the dresser and put away any clothes you have for him or her. If you have a changing table, set that up too. Also, clean the house so that it's freshly sanitized. That way, you won't be frantically cleaning when you bring your new baby home and he or she won't get sick from any left over germs. Another good idea is having meals prepared for the first couple of weeks. Even freeze some things that you can thaw so that the food will last for two or three weeks. That is, if you don't have anyone to help you by bringing over anything. It will just make the transition welcoming your little one into your home that much easier.

Utilizing Your Support System

Let certain people on your list of people to call know when you go into the hospital to deliver. That way, they can plan to come and help you when you bring your baby home. Like I said earlier on, don't invite everybody over the first few weeks. You don't want too many people in your house when you're adjusting to having your baby home. Just one or two people who will be helping out. Helping you prepare meals or clean. Maybe watching the baby while you get some rest to recover from delivery.

Enjoy Your Baby!

After preparing for your baby and welcoming him or her into your home, you're adjusting to a new way of life. Don't forget to enjoy every stage! Time goes by and your little one will grow so quickly. Enjoy the spitting up, changing diapers and late nights up putting him or her back to sleep just as much as the cuteness. Soon, he or she will be in the toddler stage and you'll be dealing with potty training. Enjoy it all! You only get one chance at them being small. So make the most of it!

# Conclusion

Having a new baby is an exciting and stressful time for many. From all of the symptoms you will experience physically to all of the emotions you will experience that will mentally weigh on you, there is a lot you will go through. It is important that you brace yourself for everything that is to come.

Having this audio guidebook is a great way to recognize what symptoms are normal, and which are alarming. You can also prepare yourself for each trimester, and ensure that you are taking the best possible care of yourself. Even though pregnancy is a largely physical experience, you should also do your best to slow down and enjoy it. This may not be easy, especially if you are experiencing difficult symptoms or a high-risk pregnancy, but it is important since this experience is one you only get to have once in a lifetime.

It is important that you prepare yourself for childbirth well in advance, and that you maintain open lines of communication with everyone involved. The more open you are and honest you are about how you are feeling, the easier this process will be for you.

Most importantly, stay calm and relaxed as much as possible, and nurture yourself in every way that you can to make this process as easy and as comfortable for you and your baby as possible.

Lastly, if you enjoyed this audiobook I ask that you please take the time to review it on Audible.com. Your honest feedback would be greatly appreciated.

Thank you.

Now, I would like to share with you a free sneak peek to another one of my audiobooks that I think you will really enjoy. The audiobook is called "Self Compassion: The Mindful Path to Understand your Emotions" by Kirstin Germer, Christopher Neff and it's A Practical Guide to Learn the Proven Power of Self-Acceptance, Self-Criticism, Self-Awareness and Mindfulness. You will also learn how to be Kind to Yourself and Move On.

Enjoy!

# Introduction

Fostering a sense of self-compassion and self-acceptance can be challenging even for a healthy and well-rounded adult. Despite how important these two characteristics are, very few people are taught about how to utilize them in their personal lives. Instead, we are often taught to be hard on ourselves, push ourselves as far as we can, and demand the maximum results out of our efforts. While challenging yourself to achieve substantial growth is valuable, pushing yourself to the point where it becomes self-sabotaging is not a positive habit to support.

If you truly want to achieve all of the success that you desire in life, you need to have a clear understanding of your mental wellbeing and around how you can support it so that you can improve your chances of succeeding. Without a strong mindset to back them up, most people will fail to achieve their desired level of success because despite having the best of intentions, they will struggle to keep themselves focused and motivated. Through the emotional and mental self-sabotaging behaviors such as having an overly harsh inner critic or trying to push through challenging emotions without acknowledging their purpose or healing them, they will simply burn out and fail to thrive.

As you listen through this audiobook, realize that you are going to be granted every single tool you need to begin developing the skills to become more self-compassionate and self-accepting. From identifying how to feel your emotions and develop a relationship to building a productive mindfulness and self-awareness practice, everything is devoted to helping you motivate yourself in a healthy way. The tools in this audiobook will not encourage or motivate you to become complacent, lose focus, or stop aiming for your dreams with any less intensity than you already have been. Instead, they will support you in having a stronger focus on how you can achieve your goals without compromising your inner sense of wellbeing. As a result, all of the success that you earn in your life will feel far more meaningful and positive.

If self-compassion has been particularly challenging for you until now, or if the concept itself seems foreign, I encourage you to really set the intention to approach this audiobook and the subjects within it with an open mind. You will get the most out of each chapter and all of the tools provided if you give yourself permission to see things from a new perspective at least for the duration of this audiobook. Fully embrace the practice of not only learning about and understanding these concepts and tools but actually working towards putting them into practice in your life as well. As you begin to see just how powerful they are and how they support you in moving forward towards a more positive future, you will quickly begin to realize why they matter so much.

Lastly, there is one major concept that you need to realize before you begin listening this audiobook. That is — self-compassion is an act of self-care, but it is also a tool that is learned through personal development practices. You are not going to be able to achieve self-compassion all in one attempt, nor will you truly be able to measure or grade yourself on the level of self-compassion that you currently have or that you develop. While there are ways for you to track your improvements and we will go into detail on those ways later, you need to understand that this practice is solely about helping yourself feel better and feel more positive in your approach to life. By allowing yourself to embody that balance, you will begin to feel far more peaceful overall.

Now, if you are ready to embark on the next chapter of your journey in self-development, it is time that you begin! Remember, self-compassion is a powerful tool for you to equip yourself with, so approach this audiobook as open-mindedly as you possibly can. And of course, enjoy the process!

# Chapter 1: Understanding the Self

Your Self or your identity is an important element of who you are. When you consider who you are, the illusion that you come up with is how you identify yourself. Although we tend to believe that our selves are an inherent part of who we are and that our personal beliefs over ourselves are finite and final, the reality is that who we are and who we think we are, typically reflect two entirely different people. Many people fail to realize that there is a difference and often find themselves genuinely believing that they are the person whom they envision in their minds and that there is no other alternative or option. As a result, they may end up developing a highly toxic, unrealistic, and self-sabotaging image or belief around who they are.

Realizing that who you truly are and who you think you are is two different people can come as a sense of relief to many. When you discover that there is a good chance that you do not actually align with the images or beliefs you have created, you realize that there is an opportunity for you to see yourself in a new light. You may even get the opportunity to start seeing yourself more clearly for who you really are, rather than for the illusion that you have been holding onto in your mind. In fact, by detaching from the strict identity you have held onto in your mind, you can give yourself the opportunity to begin experiencing far more compassion towards yourself in your life.

Identity is a rather complex topic that extends far beyond the image we carry of ourselves and the image that other's carry. In fact, there is an entire psychological study devoted to understanding identity and your sense of self and helping you discover exactly "who" you are. This field of study is known as social science and is comprised of psychologists and researchers who are actively seeking to understand identity to an even deeper level and get a clear sense of what makes a person's identity. Because there are so many different levels of identity, the study itself is quite expansive and continues to discover what one's true identity is versus the way they identify themselves and the way others identify them. In the following sections, you are going to get a deeper insight into what your sense of self truly is, how it is made up, and how your sense of self impacts the way you live your life.

## Discovering the Multiple Selves

There are two ways that people have multiple sense of self. The first way that you can experience multiple senses of self comes from how you interact with the people around you and the identity you possess around these people. For example, the self you are around your friends is likely quite different from the self you are around your family or your co-workers. Your environment is a huge factor in which role you will play, depending on where you are and who you are actively surrounded by. The second way that you experience multiple social selves is determined between the way you perceive yourself and the way others perceive you. Since everyone has had their own unique interactions and experiences with you, it is not unreasonable to realize that everyone sees you slightly different from how others see you. For example, your best friend may see you completely different from how your other friends may see you, or your Grandma may carry a completely different belief of who you are compared to the rest of the world. The relationship that people share with you, the experiences that you share together, and their perception of you and of people in general will all impact how people identify you. As a result, you actually have multiple identities – and no, that does not mean that you are having an identity crisis or that you have something wrong with you. It is actually entirely normal to have many identities.

When it comes to identifying yourself, you must realize that on a psychological front, you are not identifying yourself as one person inhabiting one body. You are identifying yourself based on the actual identity that you carry or the characteristics and personality traits that you are perceived to have. Your "self" is the conscious aspect of you that interacts with the world around you, communicates with other people, and shares experiences with others. Although there is no scientific evidence that proves that there is an out-of-body "self," most psychologists believe that the self is not attached to or identified by a person's body. Instead, it is the dimension of you that exists in your mind or the aspects of you that make up "who" you are beyond your physical and biological self.

This part of yourself that is not defined by your body or biology is typically described in three related but separable domains when it comes to psychological understanding. This means that there are three elements that coincide to make up your "self" or your identity. The first domain is known as your experiential self which is also known as the 'theatre of consciousness.' This part of yourself is identified as your first-person sense of being or how you personally experience the world around you. This part of yourself remains consistent over periods of time which results in psychologists believing that it is very closely linked to your memory. The second part of your identity is what is known as your private self-consciousness. This is your inner narrator or the voice that verbally narrates what is happening in your life to you privately within your mind. When you are reading, learning, or interpreting the world around you, this voice is actively narrating how you are interpreting that information and what sense you are making of it. This is the part of you that carries your beliefs and values about how the world works. Neuroscientist Antonio Damasio calls your private self-consciousness your autobiographical self because it is regularly narrating your autobiography in your mind. The third and final dimension of your identity is your public self or your persona. This is the image that you attempt to project to others through your actions, attitudes, behaviors, and words. This is the part of your self that other people interact with and see which results in this being the part of yourself that people generate perceptions around. It is through your persona that people determine what your identity is according to them and their own understanding.

With all that being said, the multiple selves that you embody comes from the persona that you share with others. People will then generate perceptions around who you are, what your identity is, and how they feel about that. It is through this persona that people will decide if they can relate to you, if they like you, and anything else relating to how they feel about you. In realizing that people generate their perceptions of you based off of one single aspect of who you truly are, it helps you realize that their perspective is not accurate. In fact, neither is yours. No one, including yourself, *truly* knows who you actually are. Everything is just generated based on beliefs, values, perspectives, and understandings that have been accumulated through varying life experiences.

Relationship with Ourselves
The relationship that you share with yourself often develops somewhere between the first and second dimensions of your identity. The way you interpret and interact with the world around you, combined with your beliefs and values helps you generate a sort of self-awareness that allows you to begin determining what you believe your identity is. Again, just like with other people, your identity is largely based off of your perception and understanding of the world around you and

how it works. Even if your own perception is rarely accurate when compared to who you actually are which is a unique blend of all three layers of your dimensional identity.

Because your relationship with yourself is largely defined by your beliefs and values and your ability to live in alignment with them or not, it is easy to realize that how you identify yourself can be easily shifted based on your perceptions. If you carry certain core beliefs about how people should live, for example, and you are not living in alignment with those beliefs, then you may generate a perception that identifies you as someone who is bad or unworthy. You might relate yourself to the identities you have mentally designed for other people in society who you believe to be bad too which can result in you seeing yourself in an extremely negative light. If you carry certain core beliefs about how people should live and you *are* living in alignment with them, you may praise yourself and see yourself as good and special. You might then find yourself relating more to people in society who you see as good and positive, thus allowing you to cast yourself in a positive light.

The reality is that none of us are truly inherently good or bad, we are all just perceiving, experiencing, and responding to the world around us. Generating internal images of what is positive and what is not only results in you setting standards for yourself on how you should behave. If these standards are beyond what you can reasonably achieve or do not align with what you genuinely want in life, then you may find yourself adhering to beliefs and values that are actually rather destructive. Instead of helping you live a life of contentment and satisfaction, you may find these beliefs leading to you constantly feeling incapable and under confident. As a result, your relationship with yourself may deteriorate because the way in which you view yourself is not reasonable or compassionate.

## Everyone Has Their Own Filters and Explanatory Styles

To help you develop your understanding of how your perception of yourself varies from other's perception of you, let's discuss personal filters and explanatory styles. Understanding why everyone has such different views of the world allows you to have a stronger understanding as to why there are so many aspects of your identity based on your own personas and the way that people perceive them and you. The concept of personal filters and explanatory styles is simple. A personal filter is how you see the world and your explanatory style is how you explain it to yourself and to others.

Every single person has a unique filter and explanatory style that is based on their own unique experiences in life. All of the interactions they have had, the situations they have encountered, and things they have been told by the people around them shape the way that they view life itself. How each of these small yet impactful things come together will shape how each person perceives the world around them, others that cohabit the planet with them, and themselves. So, for example, if someone along the way has learned that not washing your dishes every day is a sign of laziness and ignorance, then that person is going to believe that anyone who leaves dishes in the sink overnight is somehow "bad," including themselves.

The foundation of a person's filters and explanatory styles are rooted in childhood when a child is not yet able to generate their own independent thoughts and beliefs. Until we are six years old, our ability to critically think about things and generate our own opinions independent of the opinions of others is virtually non-existent so we absorb everything we learn. This means that anything your parents said, people around you were saying, or you were shown through other's behaviors and actions were anchored into your mind as the foundation of your personal beliefs and values. Even though you gained the capacity to think critically and start generating your own opinions around six years old, you were still actively internalizing what everyone told you because, in most cases, no one ever taught you otherwise. As a result, you likely have many different beliefs and values that stemmed in your childhood which have gone on to impact you for years to come. In fact, these very beliefs and values are believed to make up a lot of what your autobiographical-self narrates to yourself on a daily basis, thus shaping the way you see yourself. See, who you think you are may not even be an accurate reflection of how *you* think, it may actually be an internalization based on the beliefs and values you were taught by people as you were growing up.

Since every single person will hear different things throughout their lives even if they are raised in similar environments, the way that every person views and interprets the world around them varies. Even siblings will grow up to have different perceptions and beliefs based on the way that they have internalized the beliefs they heard and were shown throughout their lifetimes. It is through this process that each person develops their own personal filters and explanatory styles for how they interpret and explain the world around them. Because of this, we can conclude that any beliefs that you have around who you are and any beliefs that others have around who you are do not actually define who you truly are. Instead, they define the belief systems that you have established throughout your life until this point.

When you realize that your beliefs are what shape your *perception* of your identity and not your identity itself, it becomes a lot easier for you to have compassion for yourself. You begin to realize that how you see yourself is not necessarily a true reflection of who you are, but instead a way that you have been lead to view yourself. This view was designed to support you in feeling connected to your 'tribe' or family and community, but in some cases, it can become destructive and result in you feeling deeply disconnected from yourself. When that happens, realizing that you are not inherently 'bad' or 'wrong' because you do not feel like you fit in makes it a lot easier for you to have compassion for your feelings and for the experiences you are going through. As a result, healing from these painful emotions and moving forward into a more self-compassionate and self-loving future becomes a lot easier for you.

Thank you for listening, this preview in now over.

If you enjoyed this preview of my audiobook "The Mindful Path to Self-Compassion" by Frank Steven, be sure to check out the full audiobook on Audible.com

Thank you for listening.

Printed in the USA
CPSIA information can be obtained
at www.ICGtesting.com
LVHW090133150824
788310LV00034B/776

9 781951 266066